Praise for Greater than Great

"*Greater than Great* is a powerful, no-fluff guide to leadership that transcends titles and positions. With wisdom drawn from personal experience and practical insights, Jim Salvucci challenges leaders to prioritize clarity, communication, and legacy in ways that truly matter. From the lessons of a father's influence to the power of Occam's razor, every chapter is a masterclass in cutting through the noise to lead with purpose. If you want to be a leader whose impact lasts, read this book."

—Mike Kim, Wall Street Journal bestselling author of
You Are the Brand

"*Greater than Great* offers powerful and straightforward lessons for leadership. Jim Salvucci, in persuasive prose, argues that a leader must display authentic goodness, effective communication and cogent reasoning. Leaders who follow Jim's advice will inspire others to new pinnacles of distinction. *Greater than Great* is a must read."

—Frederick V. Moore, J.D., President Emeritus,
Buena Vista University

"This book is essential for understanding the kind of leadership necessary for our times. Dr. Salvucci delivers nuggets of wisdom arrived at through his life experience and writes in a style that is a pleasure to read. A quick glance at the Table of Contents and you will be hooked."

—Carolyn J. Lukensmeyer, PhD., President and Founder of
AmericaSpeaks; founding Executive Director of the National
Institute for Civil Discourse

"Jim Salvucci pours himself into every endeavor, and his motives are selfless. I've learned from Jim and many others that leadership is developed and ultimately mastered only through dedicated and determined study, practice, and exercise. *Greater than Great* is a multilayered and comprehensive guide for those determined to be more, create more, and give more in their pursuit of leadership excellence."

—Frederick H. Bealefeld III, former Commissioner of
Baltimore Police Department

"Whether you're a first-time manager or a seasoned leader, whether you've led teams of thousands or are an individual contributor, this book will help you become a leader at work and in life. *Greater than Great* is not a book you read once and set aside. It's a companion you'll return to, again and again, through every season of your leadership journey."

—Ali Merchant, Executive Coach, Leadership Advisor,
Founder of All-In Manager

"A leadership and linguistic triumph. A storybook of leadership in practice and a playbook for leaders to practice. A joyous read conveyed through beautiful writing and an exquisite use of playful prose."

—Dr. Nia D Thomas JP, LLB (Hons), MSc, DBA, Director of
Thoughts & Ideas, Knowing Self Knowing Others, Host of
The Knowing Self Knowing Others Podcast

"Great read! As a life coach I found Chapter 5 particularly interesting: It seems to summarize the entire science of life coaching, every discipline included!"

—Wayne Pratt, President of Motive8me, Inc., and co-host of
Knack 4 Business Podcast

"*Greater than Great* is a masterclass in leadership, seamlessly blending learning, logic, and life experience into a transformative guide for those who strive to make a real impact. Jim Salvucci, Ph.D., unpacks what it truly means to excel as a leader—not just in title, but in action.

With insightful wisdom and practical strategies, this book challenges conventional leadership norms and pushes readers to think critically, grow continuously, and lead with authenticity. Whether you're a seasoned executive, an entrepreneur, or an aspiring leader, *Greater than Great* will inspire you to rise beyond good leadership—to leadership that truly makes a difference.

A must-read for those committed to leading with purpose, intelligence, and heart. Highly recommended!"

—Rose Davidson, Podcast Host and Producer at Talking with the Experts, Podcast Coach, Judge of the 2023 and 2024 Australian Podcast Awards

"The best leaders don't just hold a title—they create impact. In *Greater than Great*, Dr. Jim Salvucci dismantles outdated leadership playbooks and replaces them with a people-first approach grounded in authenticity, integrity, and human decency. Leveraging his sharp wit and practical wisdom, he shows us how to build teams that thrive by offering a leadership philosophy that actually works."

—Lisa McGuire, Ed.S., Business Growth & Reinvention Strategist, Host of Your Passion, Purpose and Personal Brand podcast

"*Greater than Great* is a refreshing and insightful take on leadership that strips away the illusion of power and position, focusing instead on self-awareness, connection, and growth. Dr. Jim Salvucci delivers wisdom in concise, engaging chapters that are easy to digest yet packed with depth. Whether you're a seasoned leader or just beginning your journey, this book challenges you to rethink leadership in a way that is both practical and transformative. A must-read for those who want to lead with purpose and authenticity."

—Dr. Melinda Vandevort, Owner & Senior Consultant, Empowered Pathways Network, LLC

"*Greater than Great* is a compelling exploration of what it truly means to lead in today's world. Dr. Salvucci masterfully breaks down the often-misunderstood nature of leadership into clear, relatable insights that resonate deeply with my own belief that leadership is fundamentally human. This book doesn't just inform; it invites leaders to reflect, adapt, and lead with greater intentionality. If you're a leader seeking to elevate your impact without falling into the trap of rigid tactics or surface-level advice, Greater than Great is well worth your time."

—Josh Gratsch, President & CEO, Ascend Innovations, author of Pursuing Pragmatic Leadership

"Jim's concepts have the potential to inspire leaders to think beyond their current roles and consider the lasting impact they can make. They remind us that leaving a legacy that can truly change our lives and those around us is within our reach."

—Mitzi Ocasio, Owner, Mitzi Let's Think, LLC

"This book offers a heartfelt guide to leadership by showing how learning from family, experiences, and challenges shapes character. Salvucci emphasizes clear, sincere communication that connects with others' hearts and minds, using stories like his dad's resilience to inspire. He argues that true legacy isn't awards or wealth but the positive impact we leave through strong relationships and community focus. The book warns against overworking, which harms health and relationships, and stresses simplicity in logic—often the easiest explanation is the right one. With no jargon but with relatable examples, it's a roadmap for leaders who want to grow others and leave the world better than they found it. Perfect for anyone seeking to lead with kindness and purpose."

—Bernie Franzgrote, President/Synergy Architect, Kreativ Insight Consultants

"Jim Salvucci masterfully weaves together lessons from his academic and leadership journey to deliver a refreshingly honest guide that strips away leadership myths and replaces them with practical wisdom. His compelling case for human decency as the foundation of true leadership offers a much-needed antidote to the toxic workplace cultures that plague our organizations. *Greater than Great* isn't just another leadership manual—it's an urgent call to transform how we lead by valuing character over position, communication over control, and the cultivation of other leaders as our most enduring legacy."

—Adam Holbrook, School Leadership Trainer, Conflict Resolution Specialist, and Coach

GREATER THAN GREAT

How to Excel in Leadership through Learning, Logic, and Life to Make a True Difference in the World

Jim Salvucci, Ph.D.

JONES MEDIA PUBLISHING

Greater than Great: How to Excel in Leadership through Learning, Logic, and Life to Make a True Difference in the World

Copyright © 2025 by Jim Salvucci, Ph.D.

Jones Media Publishing
10645 N. Tatum Blvd. Ste. 200-166
Phoenix, AZ 85028
JonesMediaPublishing.com

Disclaimer:

Printed in the United States of America

ISBN: 978-1-948382-98-4 paperback

DEDICATION

"Every step of the way we walk the line."
—Bob Dylan, "Mississippi"

For Marie, who's been there every step (and stumble)
of the way.

x

CONTENTS

Foreword

The gold standard of leadership has started to change from what title you have or how well you've been able to play the game of climbing the corporate ladder to what positive impact you make on others—how you influence behavior.

Greater than Great: How to Excel in Leadership through Learning, Logic, and Life to Make a True Difference in the World is a guide to this new era of leadership. One that truly changes organizations into well-oiled machines whose behaviors align with their mission every day with every action.

Jim Salvucci, Ph.D., illustrates that leadership is being brave enough to think on your own, to forge new paths. He helps us answer internal questions: Where are you going? Why are you going there, and what will you do when you get there? He reminds us there is no cookie cutter answer to "greater than great" leadership. We all have singular, imperfect human lives—so what now, what are YOU going to do about it? What dent do you want to make in the universe?

Part philosopher, part comedy writer, and part professor, Dr. Sal reminds us it does not matter what scheme you come up with, what clever incentive you employ, or how many biographies of so-called leaders you've read; all of it won't increase the positive impact you have on others. It's our personal characteristics, such as integrity, that lead to our everyday behaviors that add up to impactful change. We all have it in us—the operative word being "in"—to become "greater than great" leaders. Dig into this book and find the leader you want to be.

This series of essays, anecdotes, and life experiences serves as a brilliant illustration of the characteristics of a greater than great leader and life lessons that cause us to reflect and question our own character. I urge you to read and reread these essays, then apply the wisdom contained—but only if you're looking for change, only if you're looking to be the person you want to be.

In this very entertaining and "fast read," Dr. Salvucci weaves in popular culture, a bit of science, historical figures and his own experiences with numerous and humorous looking-back tales of horrible leadership behavior and toxic work environments he personally endured.

(1) My only hope is Jim mails copies of this book to all those incompetent leaders so that they'll see the light and correct their bad ways.

(2) We all owe him a huge debt of gratitude for suffering for us, going through these learning experiences, and sharing his knowledge.

To be a greater than great leader, work on making habitual a confluence of non-quantifiable skills that center on human interaction. Practice intentional (not random) acts of leadership and start your own ripple effect in creating more impactful leaders; you'll see quantifiable results.

"Building a boat isn't about weaving canvas, forging nails, or reading the sky. It's about giving a shared taste for the sea, by the light of which you will see nothing contradictory but rather a community of love."

—Antoine de Saint-Exupéry, *Citadele*

Jonathan Rosen, Founder / (CRO) Chief Relationship Officer Collaberex - A Peer Advisory / Professional Development Community

PREFACE

Decades of observing, studying, and practicing leadership have brought me to one striking conclusion: truly great leaders aren't born. They're built through learning, logic, and life experience. More importantly, they understand leadership isn't about power or position but about self-awareness, human connection, and growth.

This book offers 30 essays, each representing the distillation of this philosophy. I've carefully selected and revised them from over 200 pieces I've published over four years through my leadership blog and podcast, *On Leading with Greatness* (jimsalvucci.substack.com). Each essay captures a crucial insight into what makes leaders far greater than the sum of their parts or the status of a title—what makes them greater than great.

This book is intended for leaders and emerging leaders who know there must be a better way and who seek better guidance than what they've found in standard leadership handbooks. *Greater than Great* avoids the pitfalls of those publications that offer clever but untested frameworks, unworkable theories, or overly complex and unsustainable schemes by providing clear, thought-provoking, and immediately applicable leadership insights. The essays cover various topics, from the distinction between bossing and leading and the key elements of all great leadership to the relationship of teaching to leading and how to transform an organizational culture.

I encourage readers to explore the essays in whatever way suits them best. Reading from beginning to end will uncover a cohesive argument across four sections. However, each essay also stands alone as a self-contained piece, allowing for individual reading in any sequence. Feel free to dive in wherever you like.

As I compose this preface, I realize the release of this book will coincide with my 60th birthday, which is a happy and fitting coincidence. I'm at the point where my memories, experiences, knowledge, observations, and insights are most apt to converge and forge what I hope is a spark of wisdom. This book aims to wrap up those six decades of learning into a package accessible to leaders, emerging leaders, and students of leadership across the generations.

Many of the essays explore the lessons I've learned throughout my journey—from schoolboy to university provost and beyond—and, in this sense, *Greater than Great* is a memoir. Or perhaps more precisely, it's a collection of life incidents. My background as a professor and academic executive forms the backbone of this memoir and informs the leadership insights I've gained as I evolved from an intuitive, gut-driven leader into a student and practitioner of the discipline of leadership. Along the way, these essays also touch on childhood events and other life circumstances that have shaped my views on leadership and human relationships.

My professional goal is to guide today's young leaders to become the next generation of great leaders, thereby helping to rid the world of bad leadership practices. To that end, the concluding essay outlines how every true leader's legacy contributes to this goal. Each leader generates new leaders, creating a ripple effect that compounds over time, allowing leadership to become greater than great. Achieving this vision will take a movement—one that will outlast my lifetime—but by applying the principles in this book, we can begin that work right now.

I would love to hear from you once you have read *Greater than Great*. What resonated with you? What questions or comments do you have? Have you tried applying any of the leadership principles or techniques, and if so, what were the results? Feel free to visit my website at www.guidanceforgreatness.com to leave a message. There you'll also find additional leadership resources and opportunities for continued learning.

Jim Salvucci, Ph.D.
President, Guidance for Greatness

Acknowledgements

The essays in *Greater than Great* emerged from my weekly Substack blog/podcast, *On Leading with Greatness*, which has benefited from countless supporters over the past four years. While I can only highlight some key individuals here, I'm deeply grateful to everyone who has been part of this journey.

First and above all, my beautiful and wonderful wife, Marie Sennett, the love of my life and the inspiration for all I do. Without Marie's love, my world would be a hollow one indeed.

My parents, Adele and Don, who are no longer with us. Their unconditional love and steadfast example informs so much of what appears in these pages.

Cynthia Lyons, my aunt and maternal surrogate. Aunt Cynthia volunteered to read an early draft, a delightful and loving surprise that boosted my spirit and gave me the confidence to continue.

My best and oldest friend, Geoff Winikur, who's had to put up with me since our first day in college together. His example inspires much of my thinking and writing.

My brother and sister-in-law, Paul and Sue Salvucci, who kept the faith even when mine waned.

My nephew and godson, Greg Salvucci, whose encouragement meant more than he can know.

Sally, Keenan, and Zeke Dworack-Fisher, whose love and confidence in me eludes explanation.

Anne and Luc Scholl-Feidler, dear friends who have offered support at critical times.

Aliza Freedman and Theresa Cifali, two brilliant coaches I was lucky enough to work with at critical times. Their guidance and lasting friendship has moved me further along in my pursuits than I ever could have achieved on my own.

Marty Olgunick, one of the biggest boosters of my writing over the years. He was the first to urge me to collect my essays into a book.

Chris Zaccaria, almost a family member and an entrepreneur who was an early subscriber and supporter of my blog/podcast, which helped keep me going.

Carolyn Lukensmeyer, who helped me make the transition from academia to author, speaker, and coach.

Jonathan Rosen, an extraordinary entrepreneur and connector who kindly penned a generous Foreword that I will forever treasure.

Fred Moore, former university president, and one of the few bosses I ever had whom I would call a true leader. The influence of his leadership (along with several examples) appears throughout these pages.

Dr. B.J. Fogg and Linda Fogg-Phillips, whose guidance as I studied B.J.'s Tiny Habits method proved invaluable. Not only did Tiny Habits help me develop the discipline to write regularly, but B.J.'s philosophy is sprinkled throughout this book.

Mike Kim, whose mastermind group helped me transform how I perceive my business and led directly to my decision to write this book.

Josh Gratsch, a young CEO and superb blogger (*Pursuing Pragmatic Leadership*). Our philosophies mesh in ways that defy our disparate backgrounds.

Dr. Nią Thomas, another blogger and podcaster (*Knowing Self-Aware Leadership*), whose thinking always snaps me to attention.

My coaching clients, whose success after heeding my unorthodox advice has shown that perhaps I know what I'm talking about even when I've doubted it.

My subscribers and readers throughout this journey. Without your regard, I would have stopped writing a long time ago.

Everyone who didn't make it into this section but deserves to be here. Thank you.

Introduction: A Legacy of Leadership

"As great as you are, man.
You'll never be greater than yourself."

—Bob Dylan, "High Water (For Charley Patton)"

Leadership runs in my blood—quite literally. My father, an ordinary man in most senses, was a leader in the truest sense, often stepping forward even when he held no formal title. His life could serve as a masterclass in leading by example, and his legacy shapes my philosophy to this day.

My father's early life was rough. He grew up in a home where warmth and affection were scarce. His father was distant, and his mother made it painfully clear that my dad was neither expected nor wanted. He spent much of his childhood at his Aunt Laura's home in Philadelphia's Overbrook neighborhood, where his older female cousins doted over him, showering him with unconditional love. There, he learned one of life's most powerful lessons: the importance of love and connection.

Drafted into the infantry in 1953, my father was on a ship bound for the Korean War when the armistice was signed. He remained in Korea until 1955, a precarious time when the war was no longer officially "hot," yet the fighting continued. He rose to corporal and was assigned a contingent of men. Once, after days on patrol without rest, his unit returned to camp only to be ordered back out by a sergeant. My father knew his men were at their breaking point and argued for their reprieve, suggesting other, more rested units take their place. When the sergeant refused, Dad went around him to get his men the rest they had earned.

Furious at being undermined, the sergeant vowed my father would never receive another promotion. True to his word, he assured my dad left the Army as a corporal despite recommendations for promotion to sergeant. Dad wasn't particularly proud or ashamed of his service—he rarely spoke of it. But he carried one reward from that time: he married my mom in September after returning home.

One of the first lessons I learned from my father came in fifth grade at St. Chuck's Catholic School. One of the nuns, whom we nicknamed "Mean Jean," was a sadistic enforcer who relished giving us meaningless punishments. Her favorite was assigning us pages of textbooks to copy as penance for the most minor of infractions, like talking during class or remaining silent when someone sneezed. Once, she punished us for saying "God bless you" in response to a sneeze!

One day, I was in a group that was in trouble for admitting we hadn't studied for a science quiz—even though I'd scored the highest grade. We had to carry all our books home as part of the punishment. This wasn't a big deal for kids with rides or who lived nearby. But I lived well outside the parish boundary and had my bike that day. I couldn't fit all the books in my bag, so I had to walk my bike home, dropping books along the way. It took me over an hour.

My parents were furious. As luck would have it, there was a parent-teacher meeting that week. Toward the end, Mean Jean tried to slip away from the crowd, but my father confronted her in front of everyone. You have to understand that most parents were terrified of the nuns. But Dad smelled a bully, and he never let bullies off the hook.

My parents never mentioned it to me, so I found out the next day when the kids at school were buzzing with the story their parents had come home with. For one bizarre, glorious day, I was the popular kid. Better yet, we never received another bogus punishment from Mean Jean. That day, my father taught me that bullies deserve no protection, no matter their status.

Around that same time, my father ran for election to lead his large printing pressmen's union local in Philadelphia. He had little ambition for the job but hated how poorly the local was being run and had a vision for change. He won—twice—and implemented sweeping reforms while leading negotiations during a volatile time for the industry.

Early in his tenure, he received a call from someone offering the same "support" he had provided Dad's predecessor. Dad didn't take long to realize the caller was connected to the mob.

My father told him, in no uncertain terms, never to call back. That took guts, especially for an Italian-American in the 1970s. The mob got the message—they never contacted him again.

Even in retirement, Dad was a leader. After moving into a senior living community with Mom in 2006, he organized charitable activities and advocated for improvements in their dining facilities. Later, after Mom passed away, he moved into assisted living during the height of COVID. Lockdowns were frequent and the staff stretched thin. While some aides were wonderful, others were cruel.

Despite his frailty and fear, Dad found the courage to speak up about mistreatment—not for himself but to protect others. It was now my turn to advocate for *him*, but his unyielding spirit made it possible. Even confined to bed, he was leading.

That was Dad. He always stood up when others stayed quiet—even when he couldn't sit up on his own. Though not a tall man, he towered over so many of his supposed betters. He was incredibly generous—my mom might say "to a fault"—but he filled the lives of those around him with immeasurable riches.

Throughout this introduction, one thread binds these stories together. It's not just how tough my father was or how he loathed bullies. It's how deeply he loved people, especially his family. He fought bullies because they hurt others. He helped because someone needed help. He fought injustice because it was unjust. And he loved us all enough to lead the way.

Dad was something rarer than great. He was truly good.

* * *

Greater than Great is about how leaders who strive for great-ness can leverage goodness and human decency to rise above title or position.

Think of a chessboard. The king is the most critical—the game lives or dies with him. But imagine an ordinary pawn outgrow-ing the king—not in power or position but in character. The king keeps his authority and fancy crown with its little cross, but what if a humble pawn—short in stature and sporting its bowling-ball head—could quietly surpass the king in decency and worth? Not to overthrow him but to exemplify something greater.

To be better. Greater than the greatest.

That's who my dad was and who you can be as a leader.

Each chapter of *Greater than Great* is a standalone essay on a specific aspect of leadership. While you can read them in any order, I recommend starting at the beginning and reading cover to cover. This way, you'll gain a deeper understanding as the argument builds. But either approach works. Wherever you are on your leadership journey, let this be your first and most important lesson: being good can make you greater than great.

Section 1: It All Starts with Human Decency

The foundation of leadership is simple—a commitment to human decency. In fact, the principles of leadership are also rather simple.

The challenge is implementing and adhering to those principles. But let's start with the most basic of leadership basics: be good.

Chapter 1: Just Decent Is More than Enough

> "[T]here are two races of men in this world, but only these two—the 'race' of the decent man and the 'race' of the indecent man. Both are found everywhere; they penetrate into all groups of society. No group consists entirely of decent or indecent people."
>
> —Viktor E. Frankl, *Man's Search for Meaning*

Decent. Now there's a slippery word. "Decent" is often synonymous with mediocrity. A decent grade? Well, a C will suffice—acceptable, but hardly worth celebrating. Your team has a decent chance of winning? Don't bet the farm on it! A decent song? You won't skip it, but it's not making your playlist, either. A decent restaurant? Fine if it's nearby, but it's not worth a long drive.

Decent is just that—acceptable. Good enough, and nothing more.

But what about the other way we use the word? When it comes to character, "decent" takes on an entirely different meaning—suddenly, it becomes high praise. Calling someone "a decent human being" is a genuine compliment. It speaks to their integrity, honesty, and an inherent goodness of spirit. You may not agree with a politician's every policy, but you might still vote for them if they come across as a fundamentally decent person.

You can even say that an altruistic actor is merely a decent performer but still a decent human—without fear of redundancy or contradiction. On one hand, they may be a mediocre thespian; on the other, they are guided by a strong moral compass.

So, we have "decent" meaning "meh" in one context and "decent" meaning "mensch" in another—"less than good" versus "better than good." I told you, this word is slipperier than an eel!

When it comes to leadership, decency is the hallmark of excellence. Therefore, a leader with decency must be much more than a merely decent leader.

Now, let's take a look at a couple of real-life case studies that exemplify what I think is truly decent.

In the first example, we have a longtime CEO in her last few months before retirement. She's a woman of deep conviction and honesty—a genuinely good person and an exceptional leader—so we'll call her "the Doyen of Decency."

Some months earlier, she brokered what seemed like a transformative deal with a vendor. The agreement promised to elevate the company's economic standing without compromising its core mission. She and her team had conducted thorough due diligence before signing the multi-year contract, and everything appeared solid. It seemed like a perfect way to cap off her career and secure her legacy.

But not so fast. It quickly became apparent that the vendor had plenty of sizzle but very little steak. Not only did they fail to deliver on their promises, but they also began steering the company in a direction that clashed with its longstanding mission.

This is when our Doyen really shined. She could have let things stand and coasted to her retirement, which would have dumped all the problems on her successor while preserving her stellar reputation. Instead, she got to work negotiating and renegotiating with the vendor. Finally, she decided with her team that the situation was unsalvageable, and they negotiated a contract termination, pulling the plug.

Think of the guts. Think of the integrity! She could have pretended all was well and that all those promised financial rewards were just around the corner. She could have walked away, whistling into the sunset, preserving her legacy.

No, she admitted her error. She risked her reputation by accepting full responsibility—no finger-pointing here. But in the final act of her tenure as CEO, she set things right again.

By making the tough call and taking decisive action, our Doyen of Decency demonstrated that her priorities lay firmly with the business she led and the people within it—not in bolstering her own ego. Her unwavering decency ensured she could never settle for being merely a "decent" boss. She was, in every sense, a truly superb leader.

Let's consider our second case study—an entirely different example of CEO behavior. We'll call him "the Baron of Bluster," a man defined as much by his pettiness and cruelty as by his short-sightedness. When he first arrived in town, he inherited a business in freefall. Credit where it's due, he took immediate action with his leadership team to stabilize the operation.

But after that? Nothing. Once the ship was righted, it came time to chart a new direction. Nonetheless, instead of building on the emergency measures or phasing them out when they became counterproductive, the Baron allowed them to harden into unquestionable dogma. Any attempt to suggest improvements or changes met with swift and permanent consequences. "Please deposit your head in the basket over there."

And so, the ship floated aimlessly, under the command of a status-quo obsessed administrative structure that focused more on self-congratulation, misdirection, and bullying than on true leadership.

The organization's mission had become overshadowed by the now-obsolete emergency practices. The Baron and his team sacrificed excellence—and even progress—on the altar of "that's how we've always done it." The Baron of Bluster became a paragon of fecklessness and malevolence as the business drifted toward a new crisis of chronic mediocrity.

So what lessons can we draw from these two real-world case studies? Given the effectiveness of the first CEO—the Doyen of Decency—compared to her vile counterpart—the Baron of Bluster—can we conclude that decency is more than just a nice-to-have trait in leadership?

The Doyen leaned into her integrity, which not only made her and her business more resilient but also better equipped to thrive in the face of a major setback. Moreover, she protected her mission throughout the crisis. Her organization's foundations remain solid, and it continues to be healthy and strong as a result.

In the second case, the Baron confronted his inherited crisis head-on, but he failed the test of character by clinging to the status quo. To compound matters, he relied on bluster and bullying to manage the situation, ultimately compromising his mission. Not surprisingly, his organization is floundering again. The Doyen's decency saved her organization and preserved its mission, while the Baron's lack of character led to his downfall.

As Lennie Bennett wisely said, "Excellence is the result of habitual integrity." Whether you call it decency, integrity, or character, it is the inner strength that forms the backbone of greatness in any field.

In a world that celebrates the loudest, the brashest, and the most self-absorbed, if you strive for true excellence, consider first how you can be most decent—truly decent. Human decency may seem a small thing—being "merely decent"—but when you stop to think about it, you'll realize that just being decent is more than enough. It's remarkable.

Chapter 2: Human Decency Is a Superpower

"Behold, I bring you the Superman!"

—Friedrich Nietzsche, *Thus Spoke Zarathustra*

In Chapter 1, we contemplate the power of decency, but what about the *superpower* of decency?

At the end of November 2020, during the height of the coronavirus pandemic, an emergency physician in California, Dr. Taylor Nichols, posted a Twitter thread that quickly went viral. He recounted a harrowing story from the frontlines of the pandemic—one that underscored the challenges faced by healthcare professionals, who were being tested beyond their physical and emotional limits.

Dr. Nichols described treating yet another patient who was struggling to breathe and begging for his life. As the medical team worked to stabilize him, they removed his shirt for treatment. The team, which Nichols described as consisting of "a Jewish physician, a Black nurse, and an Asian respiratory therapist," was shocked to see that that the patient's body was defaced by Nazi symbols, including a large swastika tattooed prominently on his chest. In the moment, Nichols noted the paradox that his team worked to save the life of a man whose apparent ideology of hate threatened the lives of those very same professionals.

Despite this realization, the team proceeded with their duty. They set about intubating the patient, fully aware that the procedure would expose them to significant risk of contagion. They also knew that their success in saving his life would allow him to continue spreading hatred against them, their families, and their communities. The incident illustrated the their commitment to duty and humanity, even in the face of personal risk and moral quandary.

Nazi tattoos are not some passing trend or temporary fashion choice. They are emblems of a dangerous credo, symbols that mark a commitment to White supremacy and the twisted conviction that certain people are less than human, unworthy of dignity and respect. One of the tattoos that the Jewish physician recognized was the SS logo—the insignia of the elite Nazi forces responsible for orchestrating the Final Solution and overseeing the atrocities of the Holocaust.

Maybe you want to entertain the possibility that this patient had an explanation for these repugnant tattoos—that perhaps he had acquired them in prison, seeking protection from a gang. Or perhaps, in some way, he might regret them. But then one must ask, why does he have so many? And if he truly feels remorse, why not remove them or ink them out? These questions speak to a deeper issue that goes beyond mere regret and touches on a broader reflection of identity and personal responsibility.

Reasserting the Human in Humanist

In his Twitter profile, Nichols describes himself as a "humanist," which could suggest several ideas. Based on his story, I'd guess that he means he derives his morality from serving humanity rather than from the doctrines and dogma of an established religion. If I'm right, Nichols' humble commitment to serving others is a stellar example of humanist morality in action.

The narrative culminates in a moment of crisis when, exhausted from months of battling COVID and reflecting on the hatred this particular patient expresses through his body markings, Nichols hesitates.

That's the point of his Twitter thread—not that Nichols and his team heroically attended to a loathsome man they were obligated to treat, but that Nichols is human enough to waver in his physical, mental, and moral fatigue. It's a story of people pushed beyond their limits. Nichols is a skilled enough storyteller to leave the conclusion open-ended without revealing whether the team went through with the procedure. We're left to assume that they did—that they finished saving the life of this racist patient before moving on to their next case. But again, the story isn't about the medical procedure. It centers on Nichols' ethical dilemma in the fog of exhaustion.

It's a story of human decency, decently told in 280-character bites. For Nichols and his colleagues, this nightmarish scenario is just the quotidian, the day-to-day routine. Worn down, he still constantly does the right thing, the decent thing, regardless of his feelings or doubts.

His story parallels that of Jodi Doering, a nurse in South Dakota, who shared her tale of moral outrage in the midst of grotesque circumstances on Twitter and CNN around the same time. She spoke of patients who deny the existence of COVID and call her names even as they're dying from the disease. Like Nichols and his team, she continues to care for them despite their hateful contempt.

A banner on her Twitter profile read, "Be a Good Human," a sadly radical stance in today's world. As Nichols observed, simply continuing to treat patients amid COVID-19 denial and hostility toward medical personnel from a wide swath of the population is demoralizing, especially in a place like South Dakota. That's where the governor's policies contributed to the spread of the disease and openly fueled widespread pandemic denial and subsequent contempt for medical professionals.

These tales of embattled medical professionals—just two examples of an untold number of similar stories—are more extreme than what most of us will ever experience. Still, they clearly illustrate the power of decency, of remaining "a good human," in the face of horror.

I'd go even further, though. For those of us in other walks of life, it's hard to imagine facing anger, unreason, resentment, and hatred every day from the very people we're committed to serving, whether they're patients on a gurney or governors in the statehouse. Practitioners in other professions may confront similar dilemmas (law enforcement officers, teachers, and yes, even lawyers come to mind), but perhaps not in such stark terms, with such high stakes, and under such constant duress.

In these circumstances, maintaining basic human decency—being a good human—becomes more than just a power; it's a *superpower*. It takes an extraordinary amount of fortitude to assert decency day in and day out, even without the onslaught of abuse and offense that medical professionals—these human beings—encounter. Maintaining decency and its attendant virtues of integrity and compassion is simple but not easy. It's not enough to declare, "I am an honorable person, a good human," or to merely intend to be virtuous. Decency manifests as a behavior that demands constant vigilance, a vigilance that, in itself, is enervating. This is partially why Nichols hesitated momentarily before saving his patient.

Human decency—being a good person in the face of it all—is indeed a superhuman feat. It's an act of heroism that may just save us all. While it's not as cool and fanciful as the ability to fly, turn invisible, or punch through brick walls, it remains the only superpower that challenges our humanity and, thereby, the only one that can help make us fully human.

Chapter 3: Stuff Your Ego in a Sack and Throw It in the River

"On the highest throne in the world, we still sit only on our own bottom."

— Michel de Montaigne, *Essays*

Maybe you'll want to join me as I set out on a task that will take some fortitude. I'm going to stuff my ego in a sack and throw it in the river.

The act I'm describing—as violent as it seems—is one of neither homicide nor suicide. Let's call it *egocide*, the murder of the narcissistic self. The ego.

Egocide is vital to great leadership. A leader must learn to put the self aside to serve others. And that's what a leader does: serves others. Don't worry. You can commit egocide over and over, but the damn thing never really dies.

At this point, as a sharp reader, you may object that professing to do such a thing is an act of narcissism itself. By drowning the ego, I paradoxically focus on it and thereby nurture it. Like advertisements, politicians, and Schrödinger's cat, the ego thrives on being seen and acknowledged. Even negative attention nourishes it. Certainly, if you're the sharpest of sharp readers, you'd be right, which is why this whole exercise sucks—and why it's so crucial.

Every day, leaders confront situations that challenge their sense of self and imperil their complacency. These challenges can be menacing. But what if—and stay with me here—those challenges aren't threats? What if they're opportunities for self-discovery and growth?

Now, I'll admit that these challenges could very well destroy our sense of self-satisfaction and self-confidence. But if so, wouldn't that suggest that these self-assurances were flimsy things? Instead, let's think of such challenges as a chance to stress-test our sense of identity and make adjustments, to strengthen it through self-assessment and build resilience.

The challenges I speak of are too myriad and varied to list or describe, but they're common. Most often, they arrive in the form of questions or criticism from others or occur within, as self-doubt.

Always, though, how we receive them remains entirely within our control. We have all the power.

Yup. I wrote that, and I can hardly believe it. Frankly, I hate when people say, "Don't let so-and-so bother you. You're just giving them power." Such so-called advice annoys because it shifts the burden to the victim and makes nonreactivity seem easily within reach. And we all know how hard it is not to become defensive in the face of challenges to the self. It's only natural and, to a point, appropriate.

Let's face it—other people can do terrible things to us. When I reflect on my recent past, the grievances seem to pile up. But when I'm being honest, I realize that, regardless of their source, those grievances exist only within me. In fact, a little candid self-reflection often reveals that the very people who've hurt me likely see their actions as a great service to the world. After all, they, like me, are the heroes in their own stories.

Acknowledging that reality only makes the injustice sting more. My frustration rises, and my ego—bruised and battered—swells like a welt under a bruise under an abrasion. Let it go? How could I? How dare you ask!

Nonetheless, I owe it to myself to step back. What does it matter that they congratulate themselves for a job well done when I can prove—beyond a shadow of a doubt—that they're incompetent and malevolent hypocrites? The kind of people the worst people consider the worst people. What, exactly, does it do for me?

Even as I write these words, I can feel the heat rising in my face, flush with anger and pain. But all of it is mine. Just mine. My ego. In the end, it takes every ounce of strength I have to gather my battered, bruised ego, stuff it in a sack, tie it shut, walk it down to the river, and toss it in.

But here's the kicker: my ego will be back. It might be a bit soggy, but it will return before I've even pivoted from the riverbank to trudge home. The point, though, is that I must train myself to understand that my ego is both vulnerable and invincible. It requires protection, but I also must be willing to abandon it—to drown it. It won't die, and neither will I. I won't even suffer. And doing so grants me a measure of agency over my own life, guiding my next choices.

Importantly, this exercise must happen every day, perhaps even several times a day. It must happen in my personal relationships, in my professional interactions, and sometimes even during casual encounters or when I'm simply sitting alone, stewing in my own thoughts.

A Digression Concerning a Casual Encounter

Here I am, pushing my cart up the grocery store aisle. The aisles are clearly marked with directional arrows designed to help people move efficiently without bumping into each other. And then, there's that guy—oblivious or arrogant—coming the wrong way. Worse still, the aisle is busy enough that now my path is blocked because of him. I could get angry. I could even say something. Maybe I'll subject him to a scowl he won't soon forget! I could start an altercation!

After all, I'm doing everything in my power to keep the order (yay, me!), and this guy can't be bothered (boo, he!). I could shame him for being a self-centered jerk, but then he could turn around and shame me for being a self-righteous blowhard. Or I could just seethe with anger for the next little while, hoping my wrath would somehow telepathically reach him and disrupt his smug contentment.

Or I could simply take a deep breath, look straight ahead with a neutral expression, and keep moving. Meanwhile, I'll be figuratively standing on the river's bank, watching my poor ego, trapped in a sack, writhe as it sinks under, seemingly forever. It's a goner for sure this time!

But then, as soon as I enter the next aisle, I'm already engrossed in my search for clam juice. I could ask an employee where it is, but I don't want to do that. It's just too weird—clam juice. How would that sound? How embarrassing! Oh. See that? My moronic ego is back, glowing with the self-satisfaction of not reacting to that rude jerk. It's been humbled, and now it's proud of itself—a paradox in full swing.

So that's my intention: to learn to stuff my ridiculous ego in a sack, tie it tight, and flip the bloated thing into the river with great regularity and, yes, even a bit of glee. To commit egocide with aplomb.

Egocide is something every leader needs to practice to be truly effective. No one loves doing it, and no one ever knows you've done it. And that's the point. It's your struggle, and each time you succeed, it makes both you and the world around you just a little bit better.

Wish me luck. I plan to murder the damn thing once and for all, but it'll be back like an unwanted shadow.

Chapter 4: Integrity in the Cause of Excellence

"Excellence is the result of habitual integrity."

—Lennie Bennett

The quote from Lennie Bennett at the top of this chapter is a great line. Almost everyone claims to have this integrity, but what is it, really?

Picture a wooden chair. For that chair to be truly excellent, it must have integrity. If I showed you a chair and told you it lacked integrity, you'd probably refuse to plant your fanny. But what does it mean to say a wooden chair lacks integrity?

A chair that lacks integrity is missing something crucial or isn't built right. Perhaps it lacks a leg, or the legs are different lengths. Maybe it's well put together, but the wood's flimsy, like balsa. Or let's say the wood is sturdy oak, but the chair's poorly constructed. The screws have come loose; the joints aren't properly glued. It could be that the seat and legs are solid, but the back is rickety. Any one of these flaws would scream, "Don't sit here! This chair lacks integrity!"

Now, let's be clear. A chair's integrity has nothing to do with whether you disapprove of its style or if its color clashes with your living room decor. It doesn't even have to do with comfort. The chair can make your butt ache and still have integrity.

Physical integrity, as with our wooden chair, is an objective standard. It demands that the chair have three qualities:

- Wholeness
- Solidity
- Reliability

If a chair lacks any of these elements, just don't sit down. This chair is, at best, entirely unexcellent. You might want to consider standing. It's different when we talk about the integrity of a person. Human or moral integrity is not a physical thing. You wouldn't say that a clumsy football player who gets knocked down easily must lack integrity. Nor would you say that the behemoth who knocks him down has it.

Human integrity refers to consistent adherence to a set of moral and ethical guideposts. While this is different from physical integrity, there's an important similarity. Just as with our chair, human integrity also needs to be whole, solid, and reliable.

What does it mean to be whole in this sense? Simply put, integrity is never compartmentalized, displayed in one situation but not another. At the same time, moral integrity must be solid and able to withstand the moral challenges and buffeting it faces daily; it's resilient. And it must be reliable so that others know they can count on you and your integrity.

A *Breaking Bad* Interlude

Even if you haven't seen it, you may be familiar with the premise behind the popular TV drama *Breaking Bad*. The series is as much about moral integrity as it is about cooking methamphetamine. In it, Walter White starts off as a seeming paragon of integrity: a nebbishy high school chemistry teacher who once passed up a chance for big bucks to raise a family and lead a normal life. But his moral compass softens and melts like one of Dali's fluid clocks when things go sideways. He doesn't have integrity at his core; all he has is pride and hubris.

White's character isn't solid. Faced with a major health crisis and money troubles, what's his workaround? Cooking and selling crystal methamphetamine as the ruthless "Heisenberg," his nom de guerre. At first, he does it because he needs the money, but quickly, he comes to love it. His twisted version of integrity is all about his overweening vanity. It's not enough for him to just cook and sell meth. His product has to be the best meth the streets have ever seen.

White's sense of ethics is also not whole. Although he plays the righteous family man at home, he's simultaneously rising to become a brutal drug lord on the mean streets of Albuquerque. Turns out you can't oversee a drug empire and be a loving father at the same time. He soon drags his loyal wife into his operation and gets his DEA agent brother-in-law murdered. In the end, in some perverse attempt to be a devoted father, he sets up his family financially by threatening and extorting his innocent former business partners from back in the day. Walter White's brand of integrity is grotesque.

As for reliability, his family eventually disowns him while every criminal out there wants him dead. No one trusts him. He can't even be counted on to stay in hiding and returns to Albuquerque to meet his demise and end the series.

Integrity—or its twisted doppelgänger—is also key in the *Breaking Bad* prequel, *Better Call Saul.* In this series, we dive deep into the mind of White's lawyer, Saul Goodman. He starts out life as Jimmy McGill, a young man with a severe integrity deficiency. As a boy, Jimmy even steals from the till of his father's store, growing up to become "Slippin' Jimmy," an inveterate con artist and grifter who stages accidents for money. He eventually tries to go straight and becomes a lawyer like his older brother, Charles, but his newfound integrity melts in the face of temptation like ice cream on a hot pavement. His integrity lacks solidity.

His brother, Charles, on the other hand, comes off as Mr. Integrity, a lawyer as highly respected as he is high powered, with a reputation as a stickler about ethics and the law. Indeed, unlike Jimmy, his integrity is solid, but he does not hesitate to sabotage his brother. He can't stand the idea that "Slippin' Jimmy" is trying to make something of himself in Albuquerque's legal world, the very world where Charles is king.

So, Charles' integrity lacks wholeness. It's no good to practice robust professional integrity as a lawyer but utterly lack personal integrity as a brother. Eventually, his two divergent moral codes clash, proving too much for him.

Like *Breaking Bad*, this show may be fiction, but it lays out the perils of weak or incomplete integrity. Jimmy's integrity isn't solid, Charles' isn't whole, and neither is reliable. You'd put them out for bulk trash pickup if they were chairs.

* * *

Integrity isn't merely an intention. It's a practice, a set of ongoing and consistent behaviors based on guiding principles. As Albert Camus wrote, "Integrity has no need of rules." In other words, your guiding principles must radiate from within.

Integrity isn't about being stubborn or rigid, either. That's where Walter White and Charles McGill go wrong, in being inflexible. Their rigid adherence to some self-serving internal code is based on pride and hubris. As we all know, it's the inflexible who break first. In contrast, integrity builds resilience, that ability to snap back from adversity—even when that adversity is itself the result of a failure of integrity.

This brings us back to Lennie Bennett: "Excellence is the result of habitual integrity." When that integrity becomes a habit—your go-to move—your resilience builds, and your resolve strengthens. There's no reason, then, to cut corners, deceive, or evade to get by. There's no reason to settle for the substandard or inadequate.

The practice of integrity is like that chair: solid, whole, and reliable, but have no illusions: practicing integrity consistently can be a challenge. Nonetheless, it's one whose benefits always outweigh the costs. Integrity isn't only a virtue; it's a source of quality and strength. And it's the difference between the truly excellent and all the rest.

Chapter 5: Putting Your Values to Work

"Three quarks for Muster Mark!"

—James Joyce, *Finnegans Wake*

If you're not putting your values to work, what are you doing with them?

Your values serve three purposes in your life and work that seem contradictory when taken together:

- First, they ground you, ensuring you don't go too far astray.
- Second, they direct and drive you, propelling you forward.
- Third, they provide a destination or target.

How can values do all three: *root* you in place, *push* you forward, and *establish* a goal?

It's a puzzlement, right? Our perception of values defies common sense, but within themselves, their three-part purpose is perfectly logical. Values are simultaneously stable and dynamic. They can anchor the present, move you, and set the future—all at once.

Consider Quarks

Whenever something behaves too strangely to be easily grasped—such as the triple yet divergent purpose of human values—it's a good bet that quantum mechanics will offer an apt analogy. What's your favorite subatomic particle, by the way? Mine is the quark.

According to quantum mechanics, a quark can be in more than one state simultaneously. Weirder still, that quark can only exist in two states at once if it remains unmeasured. Observing the particle fixes it to just one of the states, making demonstrating the phenomenon a bit challenging. Or so my infinitesimal knowledge of quantum physics would have it.

I don't pretend to know much about physics (ask my high school teacher!), let alone understand it. Still, my superficial take on this curiosity should be enough to help us grasp the similarly paradoxical nature of values. After all, it is just an analogy.

Human values, like particles in a quantum condition, can exist simultaneously in more than one state, but their tri-state existence collapses if observed. In other words, at any given moment, we can perceive values in one of their states—as an anchor, driver, or destination—even though they're otherwise in all three states at once.

Imagine being on a boat in a lake. If you deploy the anchor, it holds you in place. If you use the engine instead, it propels you forward. Meanwhile you can also set your destination out there on the horizon. Values are like all three—anchor, engine, and destination—but at the same time.

When considered this way, your values will serve you in any state, ensuring you're moored, progressing, and on target. These values are powerful stuff. Dare I say, they are quarky.

So, how can you put your values to work in all three states? Here's a four-part process.

1. Identify your values

Values are at our core. They're the principles that are most important to us. They just seem right. So how do we identify them?

There are several ways, but here's one approach. Start by thinking of three things:

- **What's most important to you in your life?** (Your grounding)
- **What best motivates you to act?** (Your progress)
- **What do you most want out of your life?** (Your target)

You can come to the third one by imagining yourself decades from now, at the end of your days, contemplating the great life you've led. What choices did you make to bring you such contentment? What values do these choices reflect? What do they represent?

For example, if your spouse and children come to mind as important, perhaps the value they most represent is love, family, or companionship. If you see owning a large house as important, your core values may include physical comfort, status, providing for family, or material gain.

2. Assess and edit your values

Nothing is perfect, and as important as your values are, they're not perfect either. Once you've identified your values, be sure to check in with them from time to time to see if they still make sense. Circumstances change. Perspectives change. And people change. So may values.

You may hold a value now that you didn't hold ten years ago or won't hold ten years from now. The change might be a matter of degree. You could love someone a lot now but love that person even more in the future—or maybe less, or maybe someone else.

Perhaps when you were younger, you saw hard work as a primary value, and now, as you grow older, you temper your hard work with family time. Maybe you've become more religious or less religious. Your values can and should shift over time. The key is to recognize that fact and to ascertain why. Be aware, though, that if any of your tenets fluctuate easily with new circumstances, they're not core values.

3. Embrace your values

Now that you know your values and have determined them to be the right values for you, it's time to embrace your values. Write them down. Review them regularly. They're you at your heart and at your best. They center you and help make you who you are. Think of it this way: when you embrace your core values, you embrace yourself.

4. Practice your values

It may seem obvious, but we forget all the time. The proof of values is in their practice, so you must implement your values. They should inform every decision and action you take at home or work. Core values can't be categorized or compartmentalized. If you profess a value and embrace it, you must live it as consistently as possible. You *are* that value.

All too often, people assume that because they can identify and express their values, those values are instantly relevant. They may print them on business cards, list them on their website, or even paint them on an office wall.

In other cases, they imagine that because they're value-driven in their home life, their work life is somehow exempt—that they don't have to be the same person. The truth is, though, that core values are core; they are you. As we see with integrity in Chapter 4, you can't swap values out whenever it suits you.

Who are you if you always practice a core value but for this particular situation or that specific environment? To remain true to your core self, you must always act on your values. How you act demonstrates who you are; who you profess to be does not. Through practice, we demonstrate how much we value our core values. We call this practice "behavior." Your core values ultimately manifest in how you behave.

Without consistent action, values are irrelevant.

* * *

Great leaders are all about values. They know their values, assess them, embrace them, and live them. The people around them see this and intuitively know the leader's values as well. The best people want to follow values-driven leaders because they share something at their core. Connecting through values is how we identify our tribes and how we build and move teams toward success.

Teams need motivation to move forward, certainly, but they also need inspiration to find a common cause. Great leaders use shared values to ground, inspire, and focus their people on what's most important. Without the leader promoting that shared sense, the team is no team at all—it's just a group of people working together.

Without core values, the leader is no leader at all—they're just a boss.

Leadership isn't about managing tasks—it's about guiding people toward a vision and fostering a sense of purpose. When values sit at the heart of that vision, they help to align the team, creating a shared understanding of why they're working together and what they hope to achieve. This alignment can turn a group of individuals into a cohesive, motivated team. Leaders who embody and promote these values create an environment where people don't just follow—they're inspired to collaborate with intention and dedication. That result is the very stuff of great leadership.

Chapter 6: The Politics of Possibility vs the Politics of Power

> "In political life I have never felt that anything really
> mattered but the satisfaction of knowing that you
> stood for the things in which you believed, and had
> done the best you could."
>
> —Eleanor Roosevelt, *My Day*

Welcome to my "Ted" Talk.

Two types of politics permeate most workplaces. The first is the *politics of possibility*—the idea that people can be inspired and motivated to collaborate for the greater good through persuasion and an appeal to shared values. This approach harnesses passion and intellect, bringing individuals together in a common cause for collective progress and betterment.

The second, unfortunately far more common, is the *politics of power*. This brand of politics centers on ego and operates on a zero-sum mindset, frequently relying on the machinery of personal destruction. Here, the collective "we" is only invoked in service to the individual "I." Accomplishments are seldom shared; even ostensible teamwork is often just a coalition of self-interest. Practitioners of this philosophy tend to claim credit disproportionate to their contribution, treating the betterment of the organization as little more than a means to their own advancement.

You've likely witnessed the politics-as-bloodsport crowd and the untold damage they wreak on individuals and institutions alike. Sadly, this winner-takes-all mindset is prevalent across industries. Too often, individuals prioritize self-preservation and personal gain at the expense of their organizations, clients, and even missions. Thus, the petty and ignoble politics of ego-driven self-interest thrive—and the consequences can be devastating.

But what about the politics of *possibility*—of achieving meaningful progress, maximizing success, and sharing the rewards? How can we champion and assert the power of this approach in our organizations?

Ted Talkin': Ted Lasso vs Jamie Tartt
(With occasional translations for those whose first language is American)

In the first season of the *Ted Lasso* television series, two characters embody contrasting worldviews on achieving success. On one side, we have Jamie Tartt, a young *football* (soccer) star known for his brashness—hence the name "Tartt." Jamie's approach to winning games revolves around seizing control of the ball and charging straight for the goal.

His undeniable talent as a *cracking* (supremely skilled) player makes his strategy relatively effective even though he's a bit of a *prat* (arrogant fool). When Jamie scores a *goal* (point), it's all about him. He celebrates his success as a singular personal triumph that just so happens to benefit his *club* (team).

In the *clubhouse* (locker room), he's a self-interested bully who demonstrates his lack of respect for his *clubmates* (teammates) by ladling from his bottomless well of self-regard. He neither encourages his clubmates nor celebrates their successes since—in his zero-sum mind—their achievements somehow dull his luster. For Jamie, the team is merely an accessory to his glory, a means for a winner like him to take all. If the team prevails, it's because of him. If the team loses, it's despite his dazzling, lone, and lonely play. Jamie will even *throw a wobbly* (have a temper tantrum) to deflect blame.

In the clubhouse's internal politics, Jamie commands attention through a bold mix of fear, resentment, and wary admiration from his *mates* (colleagues). Those who fail to openly revere him—or worse, those who dare to outshine him—risk incurring his considerable wrath. Jamie embodies the politics of power: ego-driven, self-serving, and reliant on intimidation and self-promotion. For him, the team exists solely as a vehicle to serve his ambitions.

The series' set-up is that the new *gaffer* (coach), Ted Lasso, is a hyper-amiable *Yank* (American) whose experience is limited to coaching *American football* (football) at a *uni* (college) in Kansas. Ted, of course, knows nothing about *football* (soccer). He, in fact, has unwittingly been brought in to fail in order to *scupper* (destroy) the team.

As it turns out, Ted *does* understand leadership and clubhouse dynamics better than anyone. His approach champions relentless positivity infused with a distinctive *cheekiness* (amiable irreverence). Through sheer persuasion, Ted introduces the players to the politics of possibility and gradually ropes them in—hence the name "Lasso." Over time, the team transitions from featuring individual players and their on-field performances to coalescing around a shared commitment to the club: "Believe."

Ted's methods both confuse and frustrate Jamie, but they also intrigue him. Ted knows that building a team isn't simply about assembling a group of individual stars and sending them onto the *pitch* (field). Instead, he slowly convinces each *lad* (player) that they can unlock their potential by working together to serve something greater than themselves. Guided by his inherent human decency, Ted exemplifies the politics of possibility and elevates it to an art form.

Ted Lasso's approach to clubhouse politics is expansive and optimistic, a world where everyone can be a winner if they *fancy* (want) it. Jamie Tartt's is insular and self-serving and only allows for one winner. In life, the most *brilliant* (very good) leaders are builders, like Ted. They're patient, consistent, and not overawed by raw talent and drive. Armed with grit, courage, and resilience, they serve their team and never the other way around. In a *switcheroo* (switcheroo), the team then becomes deeply loyal to the leader.

Leaders like Ted Lasso are all too rare in a world obsessed with achieving quick results and being instantly *chuffed* (gratified). Rarer still are the environments that enable them to thrive. Instead, the Jamie Tartt philosophy of zero-sum individualism receives praise and resources despite its shallow, nihilistic, and *barmy* (foolish) outlook.

The politics of possibility, marked by inclusiveness, collaboration, and personal humility, offers the best odds for collective success. Yet implementing and maintaining this approach is no easy feat. Society, perversely, tends to reward rugged individualists who hoard personal glory as if success were a finite resource.

Think about that: the politics of personal power—a zero-sum game—treats glory and winning as limited commodities. If you win, I lose, and therefore... This mindset justifies all manner of *shenanigans* (mischief) and destructive behavior.

How counterproductive, and yet how persistently such behavior is celebrated!

The politics of possibility provides the antidote to the toxicity of personal destruction. Bad actors, unbound by rules, often have the upper hand over those striving to do good, making it challenging to break through by practicing the art of the possible. Yet the alternative is simply unacceptable. We need to become builders like Ted Lasso—leaders who inspire, unite, and elevate those around them. Otherwise, we risk continuing to live in a world dominated by self-serving *wankers* (um, jerks) like Jamie Tartt.

Thank you for attending my "Ted" Talk.

Chapter 7: Using Radical Transparency to Manufacture Authority

"Be transparent, share your authority with your team, and include your people in making decisions."

—Elsa Núñez

I had a job in college building sets for our theater program. It wasn't my first rodeo—I had experience from high school productions and a summer job at a community theater. The technical director oversaw everything at the college but rarely left her office. Instead, she delegated day-to-day supervision to a full-time assistant technical director.

In my sophomore year, though, there was no assistant director. So, the technical director turned to me—an 18-year-old student worker—to keep things running.

Let's put this in perspective. I wasn't paid a dime more than any other work-study student. The federal work-study program determined the rate, and it was non-negotiable. I also wasn't given a new title or any official recognition. None of my coworkers knew about my "special" status. Oh, and let's not forget, I was naïve and very stupid.

Every day I went to the technical director's office to learn what needed to be done. She then charged me with passing those instructions onto the other student workers—my peers—organizing their work and keeping them on task.

If you know anything about systems—or college students—you can probably guess what happened next. Several of the student workers literally laughed in my face. They flat-out refused to do anything besides hang out during work hours and collect a paycheck. I quickly realized that running to our boss to tattle wouldn't solve the problem. Sure, it might work once, but it would also make me look even weaker than I already felt. Plus, my pride wouldn't let me admit how out of my depth I was. So there I was—stuck holding the bag.

It was a miserable year, but it taught me an invaluable lesson: having responsibility without authority is a recipe for disaster. It's like nailing someone's shoes to the floor and then asking them to fetch you a coffee. From that moment on, I vowed never to let myself be put in such a position again. Of course, if you've ever had a job, you already know how this story goes. I've had to break that vow many times since.

The Power of Radical Transparency

Decades later, as a university dean, I found myself in charge of the study abroad program. Unlike the traditional semester-long overseas experiences most universities offer, our program focused on short-term, faculty-led trips tied directly to coursework.

When my boss handed me this responsibility, I was struck by a strong sense of déjà vu. Much like my college job supervising student workers, my new role came without any formal announcement or acknowledgment. My boss didn't bother to tell anyone that I was now overseeing study abroad, so I didn't even have the illusion of his authority backing me up. Yes, I was a dean, but my supervisory authority only extended to the faculty within my school. The study abroad program, however, served the entire university, leaving me without any real jurisdiction. I clearly needed a plan, and fast.

The similarities to my undergraduate experience were striking. I could bluster and threaten all I wanted, but I had a high-stakes duty to fulfill with nearly zero power. Another similarity: although overseeing study abroad significantly increased my workload, I had no additional title and received no additional compensation.

History was a good teacher this time, and I was much wiser. My first step was to uncover every activity that could reasonably fall under the "study abroad" banner at our university. What I discovered was alarming.

For instance, I found that some faculty had independently organized summer and spring break student trips through third-party vendors without informing anyone at the university. This mean that we sent students and faculty abroad under the university's name without institutional oversight or even awareness. The liability risks alone were enough to make my head spin.

To be fair, these faculty members weren't trying to be deceitful or insubordinate. In their view, they were simply enhancing their students' educational experiences. However, my study abroad predecessor had a reputation for being both inept and dismissive, defaulting to "no" whenever someone proposed an idea. Unsurprisingly, faculty found creative ways to bypass him. To make matters worse, he kept no comprehensive record of even the trips he had sanctioned. The bottom line was that we had no idea how many students, faculty, or staff went abroad.

My task was to get all these people on the same page, or at least in the same book. The obvious and typical way to do so would be to create a new system (complete with forms and processes) that would control our study abroad offerings and protect our students, faculty, and the university. I could whip all that up in no time and have it in place right away.

I also knew that such a system would fail. Imposing new bureaucratic restraints would simply encourage the faculty to continue to find workarounds, and frankly, they were really good at the workarounds.

Instead, I turned to my old friends—transparency and openness. I gathered every faculty and staff member interested in study abroad (except my feckless predecessor!) for a big meeting. It took tremendous effort and all the goodwill and political capital I could muster to get these people in a room together.

Predictably, most of the faculty showed up feeling surly, untrusting, and even hostile. They expected me to shut down their trips or impose heavy restrictions. It took transparency and incentives to get them into the room, but I knew that only radical transparency could seal the deal.

I started the meeting by assuring them that I had no intention of shutting down any of their trips or programs. Combined with my reputation for honesty and straight talk, this immediately relieved much of the tension. Then, I leveled with them about my limited authority over their activities and how I knew they could easily circumvent my efforts. Since they ostensibly had the best intentions, I appealed to their professionalism by explaining the risks to the students and the institution if we continued without proper oversight. My extreme forthrightness disarmed them, and much of their hostility dissipated in that room.

That's the magic of radical transparency. I played it straight and made myself vulnerable with warts-and-all candor, and in doing so, I built instant trust. We decided to create an advisory board for study abroad and welcomed anyone inclined to participate. The goal was to set people up for success by having them collaborate. The group was large and just kept growing.

In fact, it was the only academic committee I was ever involved with (or heard of) that people continually asked to join!

We worked on projects, like planning our first-ever study abroad fair, where all these people could strut their stuff. We also reviewed case studies of student trips gone bad at other universities and planned how we'd handle a crisis, which came in handy when one of our trips met with disaster, a tale I tell in Chapter 11.

To make it all work, I continued to practice radical transparency while leaving individual autonomy intact. If someone wanted to run a trip their way, I let them so long as they gave me their itineraries and rosters and used the business office to collect and disperse funds. If I thought someone was going about it wrong, I didn't chide them or penalize them. Instead, I partnered them with a trusted peer to teach them best practices.

The study abroad program grew even more robust. It was way more than I could handle, but the giant (and ever-growing!) committee kept it in check. It was a big, wonderful mess, and it worked!

What I Learned

One key takeaway from both experiences—from my time as a student and later as a dean—is that assigning someone responsibility without authority almost always sets them up for failure.

Another important lesson is that radical transparency, allowing others to see your vulnerability fully, is a powerful strength.

By practicing radical transparency, I established enough authority to get everyone on board with the study abroad program. Otherwise, it would have ended like my experience in the theater scene shop in college—with me holding the bag and everyone laughing.

Responsibility without authority is a disaster. If you're a manager or aspire to be one, never, ever put anyone in that situation. If you find yourself stuck with a terrible boss who subjects you to such abuse, consider embracing the chaos and turning your greatest disadvantage into an advantage. Own the situation openly. Radical transparency—courageously sharing your vulnerability—can be a powerful tool to build trust, win allies, and self-generate authority while maintaining integrity.

Section 2: It's Not Who You Are but How You Act

Of course, you're a decent human being. But do you consistently behave with human decency? Do others have to look into your heart and motivations to dig up some nuggets of goodness, or do you make it evident in how you act?

It's not enough to be good inside to be a great leader. You also have to actively not be bad.

Chapter 8: Being Good Deep Down Is Not Good Enough

"He knows if you've been bad or good
So be good for goodness' sake!"

—Haven Gillespie, "Santa Claus Is Coming to Town"

When people say someone is "good deep down," what does that really mean? Does anyone ever say that about someone who is behaving well? *"Liz often gives to charity and helps bathe people in hospice care, but you have to understand that deep down inside, she's actually a good person."* That sounds absurd, right?

No, to say someone is "good deep down" is to damn with faint praise. It means that this person behaves awfully. No matter how pure and angelic their soul or whatever potential for redemption remains, they regularly act like a jerk. The consequences for everyone else can be devastating.

* * *

"Filbert is a bit of a nut," his long-suffering wife would quip with a nervous little titter. She usually repeated her pun right after Filbert had pulled "one of his stunts." His friends had a similar way of deflecting his boorish behavior. They'd shake their heads and proclaim, "That's just Filbert being Filbert," as if his rudeness and out-and-out abuse were an endearing eccentricity.

For his part, Filbert proudly relished his reputation as a hardboiled executive who tormented his employees and colleagues. He spread anxiety and misery to all who worked for him. Meanwhile, his own bosses just swept aside the frequent reports of his toxicity because, as far as they were concerned, "He gets results." Filbert didn't have to change because no one ever expected him to, least of all himself.

Over decades, Filbert had calcified into an institution around the office, which is why everyone was so shocked when he finally bit the dust. Can you believe it? A hit-and-run right in front of the building. One witness said they recognized an exemployee behind the wheel, but the cops came up with nothing. More than likely, the cosmos just exacted a bit of long-overdue justice. Whatever the case, Filbert's funeral became a must-attend event, with a few people there to pay their respects and the rest there to make sure the old coot had actually croaked.

The highlight of the ceremony came as, one after the other, attendees stepped to the podium to offer their final tributes to Filbert. Many recounted jokey tales of his awfulness, giggling awkwardly to keep their emotions in check. To a person—perhaps due to the solemnity of the scene and in deference to his widow—they concluded with some version of, "but you always knew he was a good man deep down inside." As if scripted, his long-suffering wife would lower her tissue, smile wanly, and nod slightly. Filbert, bless him, would have never been so charitable.

But was it true? How could someone who regularly mistreated everyone have been "good deep down?" Can goodness be a mere intention, or does it require action? Can you be good without actually doing good? And what does it mean to "do good" exactly?

Let's leave the full exploration of that last question to such experts as theologians, philosophers, and Jolly Ol' Saint Nick. At a bare minimum, though, "doing good" means sharing goodness with the world. It doesn't have to be some grand gesture like serving meals at the local shelter every weekend or giving half your fortune to charity before you die. Sometimes, it's as simple as flashing a supportive smile when needed or just showing a little unexpected kindness.

I would contend, though, that you can do good without being good. Many people ladle soup at the shelter every Sunday out of genuine compassion. But others do it to assuage their guilt about being jerks the rest of the time. Cruella during the week and Lady Bountiful on weekends. Are they "good" people with horrible habits or bad people who sometimes do good things?

I've worked with people who would travel to impoverished countries for church-led humanitarian projects only to return and go right back to their regular agenda of self-serving deceit, loud recriminations, and gratuitous bullying. Whatever do-goodery they mustered during their overseas visits never survived the flight home.

Let's be clear here, though. No one is good at all times and in all situations. Being good means behaving in ways that contribute positively to and better the world. As with all things worth doing, good people strive for consistency, not perfection. It's also important to note that we're focusing on overall behavior, not spiritual questions of whether someone can be redeemed or saved.

So, what about the late Filbert? Was he truly good "deep down inside," as his eulogizers alleged, or were they just being nice in front of his widow? After all, funerals aren't known for their honest reckoning. I've never been to one where someone says, "That shitbird was a total bastard, through and through," but I've been to a few where such candor would have been a relief. What if, for all his bluster and bullying, Filbert had a cache of goodness at his core? Would that be enough to say he's a good man?

I'm arguing that to be good, your actions must be good. It's not enough to be good in your heart or intent. Those good actions must be a feature, not a bug. If so, Filbert the Fearsome was what everyone at that funeral knew him to be even if they wouldn't say it: a rat down to his soul.

But let's play devil's advocate for a bit. What if Filbert didn't behave like a jerk at work but never did any good? What if, as a boss, he did nothing to hinder his employees but also didn't protect them from his noxious fellow executives? Would merely not doing bad make him good?

Not really. Neutrality isn't goodness, even if you harbor goodness in your heart. As Marcus Aurelius noted, "You can also commit injustice by doing nothing." And standing by isn't the leader's way.

So, here's another scenario. Let's imagine Filbert as a sort of Jekyll and Hyde. What if he were a sweetheart at home but a bastard at work? Would Filbert, the loving family man, offset Filbert, the nightmare boss?

No surprise here. However much love Filbert showered on his family, it could never erase or make up for the pain he poured down on his employees. As we discuss in Chapter 4, you can't compartmentalize true goodness. It's not a part-time gig or a trait you toggle on and off. Goodness, as a form of integrity, must be whole—an all-encompassing way of being.

Don't Be Like Filbert

How can we avoid acting like Filbert? We can start by identifying the rules of goodness.

True Goodness Rule Number One:
To be good, you must always strive to do good, not just intend to be good or mean well, but actively and consistently try to do good.

Come to think of it, that rule covers it. That's the only rule.

Goodness isn't some secret you conceal or hoard for yourself. It's not an intention or an aspiration. It's a practice, a habit, a way of life.

Do you feel goodness in your heart and are sure you're good to your core but never manifest that goodness in your actions? Sorry, but you're not good. If you mean well but others can't perceive or experience your goodness regularly, again, you're not good. You're not truly good if you're a perfect angel here and a howling hellhound there.

You can do good anonymously and be a good person, but you can't claim to be a good person while doing good *anomalously*—meaning, performing good deeds in a way that's out of the ordinary or inconsistent with one's usual behavior.

Now you know how goodness works. Wanting to be good, imagining you're good, or being "good deep down" while acting like a jerk isn't goodness—it's just wasted potential.

Think about this: what does being good mean to you? How often do you let others (or yourself) off the hook for bad behavior because they "mean well?" It's time for us all to stop making excuses and focus on making a positive difference. After all, this planet could always use fewer Filberts a little more genuine goodness. Could there ever be too much?

Chapter 9: Recognizing the Signs of BUI—Bossing Under the Influence

> "Power tends to corrupt, and absolute power corrupts absolutely. Great men are almost always bad men, even when they exercise influence and not authority: still more when you superadd the tendency or the certainty of corruption by authority."
>
> —John Dalberg-Acton, 1st Baron Acton (Lord Acton)

Why does the power of having power so overpower bosses?

A 2017 article by Jerry Useem in *The Atlantic*—provocatively titled "Power Causes Brain Damage"—examines studies that suggest leaders in their climb to power may lose critical mental faculties, particularly the ability to empathize and understand others.

The headline isn't just metaphorical. The brain damage might literally be real. Useem references Dacher Keltner, a UC Berkeley researcher who discovered that people in positions of power "acted as if they had suffered a traumatic brain injury—becoming more impulsive, less risk-aware, and, crucially, less adept at seeing things from other people's perspectives." (This researcher's other findings also seem to confirm what I've long suspected: that owners of expensive vehicles are likelier to drive like jerks.)

Useem cites another study led by Sukhvinder Obhi. His team employed brain scanners to show that a neural process associated with empathy—an essential quality for effective leadership—appears to be "anesthetized" in those with power. In this case, power is less like brain damage, which is difficult or impossible to reverse, and more like a debilitating drug, suggesting that power-drunk bosses may, in fact, be able to sober up.

Let's call this power-inebriation "BUI"—*bossing under the influence*—which, like its more familiar counterpart, DUI (*driving under the influence*), can have far-reaching consequences. Just as a drunk driver may cause vehicular mayhem, accidents, injuries, and even death, a boss careening through the workplace blotto on power can wreak havoc both inside and outside the office.

You can think of it as drunk bossing, where leaders intoxicated by power regularly spread anxiety and misery at work—misery that workers inevitably carry home with them. In extreme cases, jobs are lost as businesses collapse and employees flee.

Rampant employee turnover is a solid indicator of executive BUI.

So, how do you know whether your boss is drunk on power and bossing under the influence? Considering how pervasive it is, the prudent approach is to assume your boss is BUI from the outset. In fact, rather than scrutinize for signs of BUI, search for indications that your boss might just be one of the very few sober ones maintaining their human decency despite the intoxicating effects of authority and power. In that spirit, here are eight clues that your manager *isn't* bossing under the influence:

1. **Demonstrates empathy:** True empathy among managers is a rarity. The sincere desire and ability to understand others' perspectives, both conceptually and emotionally, separates the elite leader from the common boss.
2. **Delegates effectively:** A truly capable leader defers to others and delegates work and opportunity. Delegation isn't dumping work but is a demonstration of trust in and respect for the team.
3. **Avoids controlling behaviors:** Sober-minded managers don't indulge in such controlling activities as micromanagement, secret agendas, employee monitoring, unreasonable demands for overwork, and other displays of perfectionism or workaholism.
4. **Leads with humility:** Interactions pursued with modesty—where the manager does not dominate discussions and presides over an inclusive and open sharing of ideas and questions—indicate a leader

who values and trusts others. Try this test: imagine a stranger walking into the middle of a staff meeting where you work. Would they immediately be able to identify who's in charge? If not, your manager may be a humble leader or, at least, may aspire to be.

5. **Starts with "yes":** The manager who always starts with "yes" is no pushover. They're simply receptive and open to suggestions and ideas. Starting with "yes" does not necessarily mean ending with "yes," but it sets the tone for a team that genuinely values the contributions of each member.

6. **Seeks and responds to feedback:** True leaders seek and welcome honest feedback; they listen to it, and adjust accordingly. This trait sharply distinguishes leaders from mere bosses because bosses simply can't take criticism.

7. **Avoids gaslighting and bullying:** Why must this be said? Honesty, transparency, and a positive and encouraging demeanor mark true leaders. In contrast, bosses prefer to malign, manipulate, and mistreat people.

8. **Empowers and trusts:** Only leaders default to empowering and trusting their people to do the right thing. Under such a leader, your voice is heard and heeded, mistakes are learning experiences, and you have the autonomy to do your job well. Consequently, the trusting leader then gains the trust of their people. Any other approach is mere bossing.

When you come down to it, the boss who embodies these traits isn't a boss but a leader. The leader might have a boss title—manager, director, or chief this or that officer—but they don't have the boss attitude. They don't allow the power their title confers to intoxicate them, so they're never BUI—bossing under the influence.

Power can be a tempting and potent intoxicant, but there's no need for you to imbibe. A little grit and conscious effort along with a servant-leader mindset is all you need to resist the urge to indulge. It's high time for all the bosses to sober up and become leaders. And we can all drink to that!

Chapter 10: Workplace Bullies Are Always Incompetent

"One of the boss' hangers-on
Comes to call at times you least expect
Try to bully ya—strong-arm you—inspire you with fear
It has the opposite effect."

—Bob Dylan, "Floater (Too Much to Ask)"

My old neighborhood in Baltimore, where I lived for 14 years, was known for its many bars and restaurants. We reputedly had more liquor licenses in a few blocks than in any other jurisdiction in the state of Maryland. As a community activist and a founding member of our neighborhood association's Liquor Advisory Committee, I had extensive and intimate knowledge of how these establishments operated.

We formed this Liquor Advisory Committee because, with so may bars, our lovely neighborhood would transform on weekends into a massive, raucous street party with all the attendant mayhem one could imagine, particularly when local colleges were in session.

To be fair, most of the restaurants in the area were perfectly respectable and law-abiding, and they were quite wonderful to boot. A critical mass, though, catered to the reckless party crowd and contributed to the distress of residents and other business owners without bestowing any discernible benefit.

The neighborhood association frequently confronted these owners about how they regularly served underaged and over-inebriated customers before unleashing them onto our streets. We'd explain that these same illicit customers destroyed our property, disturbed our peace, and committed any number of crimes, including public defecation, vandalism, street fighting, sexual assault, and, of course, drunk driving.

Invariably, the owners, who all lived in the suburbs, fell back on a tired array of excuses. The most common was that if the owners were to enforce all the rules and regulations that the oppressive government and intolerant neighbors imposed, their businesses would not survive, and the community would lose its vibrancy. They made this claim despite the many responsibly run and law-abiding establishments that somehow thrived while improving the neighborhood's character.

At some point I realized that the negligent business owners honestly believed that my community's peace was not as important as their bottom line. That *we* should pay the *price* for their profit. That our torment should effectively serve as a sort of tax to subsidize their shoddy business practices.

In the face of all this, I concluded that any business model that required a liquor establishment to break laws or cause undue stress in the surrounding neighborhood was, de facto, not a particularly good business model. Indeed, such a business was an utter failure because it could not legitimately turn a profit. Therefore, the irresponsible owners were definitionally bad businessmen (and the bad ones were all men).

It's the same with any business. If a company can't succeed without violating regulations, cheating on taxes, ripping off customers, or stiffing its workers, it's incompetently run.

This is a roundabout lead-in to my reflection on the relationship between bullying and incompetence in the workplace. In November 2020, a Twitter user named Richard Osman tweeted this truism that I wholly endorse: "If you can't do your job without bullying people, then you can't do your job."

Put another way, just like the feckless bar owners who couldn't operate within both the parameters of the law and the boundaries of basic human decency while still turning a sufficient profit, bullies in the workplace are inherently incompetent.

I'm pretty sure anyone who's read to this point is not one of these miscreant bully bosses I'm describing. But if I'm wrong, heed my message.

If you feel otherwise—that you can't manage well except by stepping on others—let's start with the premise that the very essence of your job is to support the flourishing of your organization. It's also not difficult to understand how bullying stresses workers, distracts them, and lowers productivity. Given all that, how would suppressing others' ability to perform improve your organization?

Perhaps you imagine that your competence is best measured by your ability to climb a ladder or retain a title. If so, consider this: how many individuals do you know who are inept at their jobs, deserve to be fired, yet have no difficulty receiving promotions?

You're likely recalling several people at this moment, maybe even your boss, right? If you know these outwardly successful people to be categorically incompetent, you can only conclude that personal success can't be the measure of competence. Indeed, despite what we're told, we don't live in a meritocracy.

Similar to those crappy bar owners, if you must break people or standard rules of decency to do your job and to get ahead, then you're not good at your job and don't deserve to advance.

I'll go further and wager that nothing in your job description encourages or even allows you to treat others badly. Therefore, if you feel your position requires you to gaslight, manipulate, backstab, harass, discriminate, bully, or simply be an asshole, then you're an incompetent individual operating outside the scope of your employment. Whether you get the work done is irrelevant in the face of your rancid behavior.

On the other hand, if you try to treat people well (and I mean *make an effort*—it's not a passive thing) and behave with decency in the workplace, then you have a shot at being competent. But just a shot. Of course, there's more to competence, but at least you haven't automatically forfeited all claims to competency by being a workplace jerk.

I'm not suggesting that you must be a perfect little Boy Scout or Girl Scout, a choirgirl or choirboy, or a passive pushover. Not at all. I'm suggesting—nay, I'm insisting—that every time you've witnessed indecent behavior in the workplace, you've witnessed incompetence at work. And if you're the culprit, it matters not what lofty title, inflated salary, or slobbering acclaim you've accrued. It matters not how big your house is, how much people fear you, or how important you're convinced you are. If you feel you need to regularly act like a jerk and treat others badly, then that's what you are at your core: a jerk.

If you don't have the intelligence, the tenacity, or the fortitude to do your job with integrity and treat others with dignity, then you suck at your job. You're a disgrace to your organization. Ultimately, that indecent ineptitude will be your only legacy. Oh, that and all the damage you leave behind.

If all this seems overly harsh or if it's hard to hear because it's a dog-eat-dog world, after all, and you need to accrue as much stuff and power as you can before you slip this mortal coil, listen carefully. There's one clear truth you need to imbibe. If you're a workplace bully and insist on remaining so, *you are incompetent*. If that hurts your feelings, as you've no doubt said to others in some form I say to you: suck it up, buttercup.

Chapter 11: Pointing Fingers Is a Fantastic Way to Avoid Solving Problems

"When a man points a finger at someone else, he should remember that three of his fingers are pointing at himself."

—Anonymous

The phone rang at 5 AM. I answered groggily and then laid back down to sleep. A minute later, I bolted upright, realizing what I had just been told: a busload of our students and faculty had been hijacked at gunpoint in South Africa!

* * *

During my tenure as a dean at a small university near Baltimore, I was tasked with overseeing our study abroad program. In Chapter 7, I explain a little of how I ended up saddled with this extra duty. My only compensation for that work, aside from the satisfaction of enhancing student learning, was the opportunity to visit a few foreign sites.

In May 2014, we sent 36 students and faculty on a five-week trip to South Africa. We were well acquainted with this destination and its intricacies, and I had personally visited South Africa twice before. This time, I delayed my departure to handle some matters stateside, planning to join the group mid-tour.

The second day of the excursion—less than 24 hours after their arrival in Pretoria—was when I received that 5 AM phone call. The students and faculty had been hijacked and robbed—a terrifying and dangerous experience—but they were now all safe and sound.

Compounding the situation, we soon learned that a student had texted home to tell their mother the story, who for some reason contacted the media. Given that one of the chaperones on the trip was our newest faculty member in criminal justice—the recently retired police commissioner of Baltimore—media interest was piqued, and we were instantly thrust into the spotlight.

I convened with the university vice presidents to determine our next steps. After a long and contentious discussion, we finally agreed it was best to bring everyone home.

None of these vice presidents had any experience with a study abroad program, and some had never been abroad themselves. One was rumored to be terrified of flying and had never even boarded an airplane. They were utterly unequipped to address the crisis.

As a mere dean, I was the lowest-ranking person in the room. Consequently, my perspective was dismissed despite my intimate knowledge of the travel conditions, topography, people, culture, and challenges. Predictably, the VPs' noxious combination of arrogance and power hampered our ability to work together on solutions, and we missed several opportunities.

The university's vice president for communications, the only VP who wasn't using this crisis as an opportunity to posture and preen, arranged a press conference with the four local television stations for the following day. She tapped me as the university's spokesperson, a role I had no training for and did not relish. Even as we worked to extract our travelers, television reporters and their camera crews descended upon our campus for a press conference with me. They set up their equipment in a designated outdoor area on that beautiful spring day.

Meanwhile, we were struggling to transport our travelers from Pretoria—where they were staying—to Johannesburg's O.R. Tambo International Airport. Normally, this process would be fairly straightforward, as the travel agency that booked the trip offered to make quick return arrangements at no additional cost. Instead, the VPs insisted on taking command of the situation themselves.

Their stupidity peaked when one VP suggested the Pretoria police department dispatch their vans to convey our travelers and all their luggage to Johannesburg. "I looked it up. It's only 30 miles," he crowed. He was the one who'd never flown. I countered that in my experience, law enforcement in any country is generally unwilling to commit their vehicles and officers to transport tourists unless it's to the pokey. He, in his boundless arrogance, remained unconvinced.

Maybe thirty minutes before I made my press debut with the local television stations, three VPs, including my boss, called me into an office for what can only be described as an ambush. They'd decided to direct their frustrations about the situation toward the trip leader in South Africa, one of my direct reports. Their gripe was he hadn't responded promptly to an email regarding the return flight arrangements and had missed the flight.

I explained that he was at the police station equipped with only a flip phone and had no access to email. Plus, he'd been told he would receive a phone call about the flight, so he had no reason to even expect and email. Nonetheless, in their minds, I was just making excuses. They simply wanted someone to hang, and he'd do nicely. Not only was their anger based in ignorance, but the optics were pretty bad. Our trip leader was Black, while all the VPs were White.

They were also indignant that he hadn't already secured a bus to transport everyone to the airport at a moment's notice. I pointed out that arranging a large bus so quickly and having it wait on standby would be nearly impossible even in the United States.

I added that although Johannesburg's Tambo airport was a mere thirty miles away, it's a massive, complex facility to navigate and often plagued with long lines. Moreover, clearance to fly to the States included security pat-downs of each passenger. All these dilatory factors would need to be considered when timing a departure.

The VPs were having none of it. One of them speculated that given the special circumstances, the airline or the U.S. Embassy would surely waive all ticketing and security checks. (I just can't make this stuff up.) The three kept hammering away at me as I attempted to reason with them and protect the trip leader.

Our exchange grew heated. At one point, one of the VPs—the one with a fear of flying—screamed, "You sound defensive!" To this day, I marvel at my restraint in not retorting, "And you're being highly offensive, you ignorant bigot!" That's what blasted through my mind, anyway.

Throughout this surreal confrontation, I could see the camera crews outside adjusting their equipment through the office window. They were ready for me. The VP for communications had come to the office door several times to retrieve me, but the other VPs shooed her away.

Eventually, it hit me that the only way to extricate myself from this situation was to allow these bullies to take out their aggravation on the Black guy in South Africa. I suggested we dial his phone from the office speakerphone and figured they'd just rip right into him when he answered. Instead, they all looked at me. Cowards. They expected me to do their dirty work.

I greeted him and then, sternly but not angrily, chided him for neither magically arranging for a bus to appear nor somehow commandeering all the police vans and drivers in Pretoria. He knew me well enough to interpret my tone and feigned indignity to make the charade sound convincing. The VPs' smug expressions signaled they were satisfied. With that deplorable exercise behind me, I was finally free to address the media with no time for preparation.

Later, after the press conference, I called the trip leader to apologize for my tone. He was familiar with the characters in the room and had understood the situation, but he appreciated my call nonetheless.

I recount this true story as an example of how the peculiar tendency to point fingers can overwhelm the need to solve problems. We faced a genuine crisis—a word I use judiciously as it's often flung about loosely to describe even routine challenges. This situation, however, was a true crisis.

With the added strain of the media scrutinizing our every move, having three VPs berate me and then compel me to reprimand my colleague (from 8,000 miles away!) was an egregious misuse of our time, focus, and energy. Even if he had screwed up (which he most certainly had not), or if I had screwed up (which I hadn't), there was no justification for indulging in this petty power play disguised as accountability.

Pausing to point fingers when a pressing problem demanded our attention was absurd. In exceedingly rare instances, assessing blame may be necessary to solve a problem, but almost always, taking time and resources to do so is a massive distraction. Furthermore, I have often found that the need to assign blame naturally diminishes after the dust has settled.

In this case, the immediate stakes were particularly high. Not only did we have to get our travelers home, but if these arrogant VPs had succeeded in rattling me, I might have flubbed the press conference and created an entirely new set of problems. Perhaps that was their goal—to set me up for failure. If so, their plan backfired.

Fortunately, the press conference went smoothly—almost. One of the local stations asked me whether we'd ever experienced a violent situation on a trip before, and I answered honestly that we had not. On the broadcast, they played my denial followed by an anonymous source—blurred out and with his voice electronically distorted—claiming the opposite. Although I was later able to correct the record during a post-return press conference, the journalistic malpractice on display was astonishing.

We eventually brought everyone home safely, albeit several days later than necessary due to delays spawned by the bosses' control-freak tantrums. As for the bullying VPs who ambushed me, they simply retreated to their offices, ready to create chaos another day.

Here are a few key lessons to take away from this experience:

- The more you're pointing fingers, the less you're solving problems. Address your immediate problems immediately. If you find it would be constructive, you'll have plenty of time later to assign blame.

- A fancy title does not automatically confer expertise or leadership qualities. Those who believe otherwise are gravely mistaken and potentially dangerous in positions of authority. Bosses aren't leaders. They're just bosses.

- If you ever have to deal with the media, proceed with caution. Remember that journalists often have narrative agendas and may not prioritize your best interests.

Let my experience remind you that true leaders focus on finding solutions rather than scapegoats. Leaders also know that there's no correlation between expertise or competence and rank. Leaders—as opposed to bosses—serve from a place of human decency so that in a time of crisis, their core values will serve them and carry them through.

Chapter 12: How I Lost My Voice

"Curiosity ... Is insubordination in its purest form."

—Vladimir Nabokov, *Bend Sinister*

What's the connection between curiosity and dissent? The U.S. is a curiously incurious society when it comes to curiosity. Not that we're not curious about things. What I mean is that we're not curious about the reality of our own curiosity. For instance, have you ever wondered why so many of us obsess over the British Royals but barely bat an eye at our own political dramas? Is William vs Harry really any more scintillating than Marge vs Alexandria?

In *Bend Sinister*, the Russian-American novelist Vladimir Nabokov wrote that "Curiosity ... is insubordination in its purest form." Nabokov's connection between curiosity and insubordination resonates with me. It aligns with my experience, particularly a childhood incident when my natural curiosity cost me my voice. In retrospect, I'm not sure I've ever fully regained it.

The Curious Tale of What Happened to My Voice

When I was a kid, I was a pretty decent student—at least until high school, when I deliberately dumbed myself down to shake off my reputation as a nerdy poindexter (which, by the way, was my actual nickname).

As a youngster, I swam in a vast and deep pool of curiosity and wanted to soak up every bit of knowledge I possibly could about the world, which is to say I was a kid. Kids are naturally curious creatures.

But that curiosity took a hit in sixth grade at St. Chuck's Catholic school. Enter my teacher. I'll call her Mrs. Boggins. She's the one who stole my voice.

As I said, like most kids, I wanted to learn. Science was my favorite. But Mrs. Boggins didn't share my enthusiasm. She didn't love science despite teaching it. She didn't love math, despite teaching that too. In fact, she didn't love any of the subjects she taught, nor did she love teaching, learning, or really any of her students.

The entire scope of Mrs. Boggins' knowledge of every subject was strictly bound within the outer covers of our textbooks. To make matters worse, those very books were ancient hand-me-downs. For instance, our science text featured a section about the Soviet Union's recent launch of the first artificial satellite, Sputnik, and how the U.S. planned to hurl satellites into space soon.

Let me put this in context. Sputnik blasted into orbit in 1957, followed a few months later by the American satellite Explorer 1. My sixth-grade science class was studying Sputnik as a very recent event nearly two decades later, years after the end of the Apollo moon program and even after Skylab, the first space station, had been abandoned.

Nonetheless, Mrs. Boggins seemed unperturbed by our grossly outdated textbooks, which is understandable. After all, her apparent mission as an educator was to ensure that her students displayed no more intellectual curiosity than she or her colleagues—which is to say none at all.

I vividly recall the precise moment of my defeat at the hands of Mrs. Boggins. It was when I did the most irritating thing that the curious—and all children—do everywhere: I asked a question. Here's what happened.

Are We There Yet? How about Now?

Mrs. Boggins was straining to explain the relationship between time zones and the Earth's rotation. She was clearly out of her depth and muddling the subject for her students. Then, suddenly, I got it! I grasped that the Earth was constantly spinning and that the time of day, measured by the sun's relative position, would differ around the globe. Cool beans!

I had an idea! Up went my hand—perhaps for the last time with such enthusiasm—and Mrs. Boggins called on me with a weary sigh. She braced herself, fully expecting an exasperating stumper. I really didn't want to confound her, but unfortunately, confounding her was unavoidable, given that "confounded" described her default state.

I asked, "Mrs. Boggins, what if someone went up in a helicopter and just hovered there for 24 hours? Wouldn't they see the Earth move below them and be able to land exactly where they started the next day?" She glared at me, her eyes fixed on my jugular as if she were deciding whether to bite into it.

But then, it got worse. Not only had I dared to display curiosity, but I'd compounded it by capturing the attention of my classmates. My innocent question instantly ignited their bone-dry stock of intellectual kindling. Mrs. Boggins would need to snuff that flame quickly before their little imaginations fully fired anew! But it was too late! In seconds, they excitedly started repeating my query.

She sighed again, looking cross, and hissed, "Why would anyone want to be in a helicopter for so long? It would be boring!" Mrs. Boggins looked rather pleased with her wet-blanket response. She clearly thought she'd successfully smothered the nascent blaze of curiosity once and for all. Her triumphant scowl mocked me.

I was mortified, stammering something about just wanting to know. She shot back her signature smirk of withering contempt.

But not so fast! The other kids were now engaged. They started shouting ways to make a full day hovering in a helicopter more stimulating. Someone suggested we send up two people to keep each other company, but Mrs. Boggins parried that then there'd be two bored people.

The kids persisted, though, speculating wildly. It was turning into a full-blown group thought experiment! What a nightmare! One clever brat proposed sending the two pilots with board games for entertainment. Everyone loved this idea, shouting out their favorite games. Within minutes, we were hammering out a consensus.

All this was too much for Mrs. Boggins. She exploded at the class in general and me in particular, shaming and humiliating me in front of my peers. Her rage boiled over to douse the flame of my curiosity.

My crappy Catholic school and its champion, Mrs. Boggins, had finally won their war of attrition against me. I fell silent, muted, afraid to speak, stripped of my voice. I wouldn't regain it until grad school when I stopped caring so much about what teachers thought of me. To this day, though, I struggle to speak up in groups and force myself to do so regularly.

I'm not sharing this story to elicit sympathy for my childhood trauma, which is admittedly mundane, middle class, and entirely first world. The real reason I'm telling this tale is to illustrate how my classroom question, for me, was just an innocent burst of curiosity, while to Mrs. Boggins, that curiosity was a form of open insubordination. In her bony brainpan, I was trying to upstage and rattle her. In truth, I just wanted to imagine, wonder, and know—the most basic elements of curiosity, learning, and (for what it's worth) childhood.

Curiosity as Insubordination

This phenomenon isn't limited to the classroom. You see it regularly in the workplace, too: a simple inquiry regarded as a form of resistance. I've been accused of insubordination on the job for merely asking, "Why?" Why are we pursuing this course of action?

Think about it. What sort of a mind is so easily challenged and sent into crisis by another's question? I'm just curious.

The association of curiosity with insubordination is perhaps why our society is so incurious about our own curiosity or its lack. Why we're so willing to let go of and even suppress the natural curiosity of our youth. Why we've designed an education system and a work culture that quash curiosity. Why merely asking questions in certain settings is tantamount to dissent.

Adults sometimes recite a proverb to instill a fear of curiosity in kids: "Curiosity killed the cat."

Well, cats have nine lives, so a single death-by-inquiry can't be all that bad, can it? Besides, the original saying is, "Curiosity killed the cat, but satisfaction brought it back." In other words, meeting your curiosity is invigorating (if not reanimating)! The fact that we only quote the first part is, I think, most curious.

I urge you as I urge myself. Recapture the shreds of your childhood spirit of inquiry. Dare to wonder—even if others think you a little incorrigible. If you're a leader, for the benefit of all, embrace curiosity—your own and others'. What do you have to lose? I just want to know.

Chapter 13: There's No Ocean There

"Swallow your pride,
You will not die, it's not poison"

—Bob Dylan, "Tombstone Blues"

Much of my perspective on the working world and leadership has been shaped or maybe warped by my experience as a faculty member and then a dean at a small university outside of Baltimore. It's a good part of the reason I have such a low tolerance for incompetent management and have made it my goal to guide leaders to greatness. This university had once been a dynamic place, but it had long fallen into dysfunction and moral corruption by the time I escaped. Therefore, many lessons I took away were "negative paradigms," an opportunity to learn from others' mistakes and dysfunctional systems.

To be sure, I made plenty of my own instructive errors, but operating in that environment was like tap dancing in a minefield while bombs dropped from above. Knowing what constituted a misstep and what was just bad luck was impossible.

In preparing for this essay, I went back and looked at my daily notes for just two months in early 2014, and I find I'm reliving the anxiety as I write. There was little remarkable about that stretch, yet the record is filled with inexplicable mistreatment, much of which I had forgotten. Reading my dispassionate account of these abuses a decade later as they pile one upon the other creates the sensation of a large mass throbbing in my chest—an alien and unwelcome presence.

My only purpose in reviewing my notes from that particular period was that it was around the time the university president abruptly stopped speaking to me for no discernible reason, a silence that lasted for nearly two terrifying years. My sole comfort then was that I wasn't the first to receive such treatment and probably wasn't the last, either.

Nonetheless, his hostility left me utterly distraught and scared for my job and career. Workplaces shouldn't have that much power over our lives.

This chapter, however, is about the aftermath—a period that proved both instructive and, I hope, far more amusing.

Even as I endured the ongoing trauma of my workplace, I was actively searching for another job because, well, obviously. I'd phrase it delicately in job interviews: "My principles were not fully aligned with my institution's practiced values." Translation? It was a non-stop shitshow.

Finally, just before Christmas 2015, I received an offer to serve as vice president at a small university in rural Iowa under a fabulous president—a real and rare leader and an exemplar of much of what I describe as great leadership in these pages.

Lo and behold, right after I announced I'd be leaving at the end of the spring semester, I encountered my old president. Instead of the usual silent treatment, he greeted me warmly. What a bizarre shock! Pretending that our relationship had been perfectly collegial all along, he immediately started quizzing me on details about my new school and its president, which was ludicrous because I had literally just been hired and knew barely anything.

It struck me that he saw my career success as some sort of feather in his cap, which was just how his mind worked. In reality, I was fleeing him and his abusive underling, my horrible boss. The president concluded that first little conversation by adding, "Make an appointment to see me just before you leave at the end of the semester. I have some advice for you."

Now, two things are worth pointing out here. One was that since I'd be staying on until graduation in May, my departure was still five months off. The other is that my contempt for this contemptable little troll was bottomless, as was his for me, so I had no interest in any advice he could offer and doubted he had any interest in offering it. Still, I thanked him and slipped away.

This scene repeated throughout the whole semester. He'd stop me in the hallway and quiz me about my new Iowa school. He was hoping to dig up dirt from what I could gather. Now and then, he'd remind me to make an appointment to get his advice. I always assured him I would, and I always made an immediate intention to forget. He kept harassing me, though, so I finally gave in and scheduled a meeting with him the Monday before graduation, the last week I'd be there.

The Friday before that Monday meeting, I ran into the president—this time in a buffet line—and he reminded me that "we have our big meeting Monday." It was difficult to understand how our appointment was such an event for him. This man who had given me the silent treatment for four semesters seemed to be looking forward to our conversation. I muttered something appropriately polite in response, and he added, "I have some advice for you." I already knew this part, so I thanked him, looking for an escape, but he kept going. "I also have a gift to give you."

"Oh," I said, surprised and slightly weirded out, "that's very nice."

"It is a book."

"Oh," I replied with as much enthusiasm as I could fake.

"Yes. It is worth between 15 and 20 dollars."

"Oh. Okay. Thanks."

What a wingnut!

That following Monday morning, I showed up for our 9:30 meeting at 9:20, hoping to get it over with as soon as possible. As I checked in with his assistant, who looked on with pity, he spotted me through his open door, waved me into his office, and sat me down. I realized that had only been in his house of mirrors a handful of times over a decade-and-a-half of employment at that university and then not for several years.

We chit-chatted for a bit as he asked some of the same questions about my new school that I had already answered, and then he jumped up. "I just remembered. I have that book for you." He sauntered over to a tall stack of paperbacks and took one off the top. "I plan to give these to all the vice presidents and deans, but you will be gone by then." He handed me a pop psychology book that he'd recently discovered, and I thanked him. So much for the special parting gift.

He sat down again, apparently very pleased with himself. "Before you go, I want to make sure I give you that advice." I braced myself. How could this still be a thing? What wisdom could this feckless sadist actually have to share? More importantly, how could I possibly get it together enough to feign interest?

He jumped right in, telling me how he grew up on Long Island and went to college in St. Louis in the 1960s. This I well knew because he obsessively mentioned it in public speeches. He then explained how he struggled to acclimate when he first moved out to the Midwest. He couldn't figure out the trouble, but then it hit him. He smiled at the memory of his adolescent astuteness.

On Long Island, he pointed out, he was never far from the ocean, but in the Midwest, he was nowhere near the ocean. I simpered politely at his lame anecdote, but he wasn't done.

He then proffered his sage advice, which he had first mentioned back in January, primed me for, and nagged me about over the past five months.

Oh, so this was it! THIS. WAS. THE. BIG. EVENT!

His smile widened: "So, when you move from Maryland to Iowa," he paused to build drama, "you need to understand that there's no ocean there." He kept grinning, waiting for my reaction. I thought he must be kidding and smiled back at the stupid joke.

He then pretended he had something else scheduled and ended the meeting abruptly. He hadn't been kidding! That was it! The advice! As I said goodbye to his bemused assistant and wandered into the hallway, I checked the time. It was just 9:30. Ten whole minutes had passed.

* * *

On my way back to my office, I reflected on the experience. Although this man had two decades on me, he lacked fundamental wisdom, a vital component of effective leadership. His arrogance and narcissism were toxic to his capacity to learn or develop and poisoned the culture of his institution from the top down.

I don't doubt that his offer of advice was sincere and that—all semester long—he figured he'd conjure some brilliant counsel at the last minute. But when the time came, he choked and could only offer an inanity. Instead of swallowing his pride and letting it go, he had to say something, anything. I'll bet he told himself afterward that he was just sticking it to me all along, putting me on, trolling me. He was like that.

Good leaders, in contrast, are constantly on guard against the encroachment of their egos. They seek to improve and cultivate wisdom in themselves and in others. They eschew personal animus, petty grievances, and churlish behavior. In short, they strive to act decently in all things so they don't just go ahead— like that guy—and make an ass of themselves for all time.

Chapter 14: Glengarry Glen Ross—The Ultimate Toxic Workplace

"Put that coffee down! Coffee's for closers only."

—Blake (Character in *Glengarry Glen Ross*)

Have you seen the 1992 cinematic classic *Glengarry Glen Ross*? If not, you're missing out on one of the most intense and brutal takedowns of the modern workplace. The film—adapted from David Mamet's Pulitzer Prize-winning play—delivers high-octane drama brought to life by an all-star cast that dominates the screen.

Set in a seedy New York real estate sales office, the story follows a group of morally compromised salesmen scrambling to close deals and secure their jobs. Their success hinges on "leads," contact information for potential clients, which they use to relentlessly pitch dubious investment properties over the phone. Survival in this cutthroat environment requires cunning, grit, and relentless determination.

The stakes escalate when management drops a bombshell: only the top two "closers" will keep their jobs at the end of the month. A vicious, dog-eat-dog scramble for survival follows, exposing the darker underbelly of competitive office culture.

The film offers a blistering critique of toxic masculinity, and we witness the corrupting influence of an environment that rewards unethical behavior. These men—and they're all men—are nothing more than low-rent grifters with real estate licenses, horrible people rendered all the more feral by the relentless pressure from management.

Ultimately, though, the movie is a study of the modern workplace and its abuses. Mamet creates a sort of closed box for the characters to operate in, which may seem artificial, but is it really so different from most workplace cultures? The television show *Severance* takes this closed-box workplace idea to its extreme, presenting characters whose work life is surgically sealed from their home life.

Even when we use the common phrase "work-life balance," we implicitly portray the workplace as a closed box, treating work as utterly separate—severed, if you will—from life. In doing so, we raise expectations for the non-work portion of our lives at the expense of our expectations for work, which can never be as satisfying. In short, each time we invoke that that popular phrase, we betray our mindset's inherent imbalance. It's actually quite insidious, as *Severance* suggests.

In *Glengarry Glen Ross*, all we see is the work side, and sordid work it is. One of the most memorable scenes did not appear in

Mamet's original play. It features a young, foul-mouthed Alec Baldwin as a motivational speaker sent by the front office. He berates the hapless salesmen, humiliating them in a profanity-laced tirade that can be summed up in four words: "Coffee's for closers only." This vicious affront masquerading as inspiration only heightens the salesmen's torment and ensures a tragic outcome.

The human element arrives with the revelation that one of the salesmen, Shelley (brilliantly played by Jack Lemmon), has a daughter in the hospital. The heartlessness of his situation, the fundamental inhumanity, seems too grotesque to be true. But it's the stark reality of millions whose employers see them only as "resources" ripe for exploitation.

The toxicity of this particular sales office is off the charts, but I've personally witnessed work environments nearly as bad. The corruption and short-term thinking of those at the top cause those below to become anxious and desperate. The ones who ostensibly succeed at this contemptible game are the ones who emulate or enable their noxious overlords. Everyone else either knuckles under or ultimately finds themselves cast aside.

Now, let's imagine what this real estate sales office would look like if it were run by competent, ethical leadership. Of course, it probably wouldn't even exist in this form since no decent, values-forward leader would ever get caught up in a scheme to sell crappy, overvalued properties to unsuspecting marks. But let's pretend, for the sake of argument, that the land they're selling is actually desirable and reasonably priced.

In this reboot, the firm's management would show genuine concern for the well-being of both the salesmen and their customers. No one would be forced to make an untoward sale, and no customer would be tricked or coerced into a reckless purchase. The office manager would strive to maximize the sales potential of his team by treating the list of good leads not as an incentive for cutthroat competition but as a resource to leverage for cooperation and collaboration.

The top seller, Tony Roma (played by Al Pacino), would still be formidable. This time though, his restless drive and gift of gab would be channeled toward inspiring and encouraging his colleagues, not lording it over them. Instead of conning leads who neither want nor can afford what he's selling, he'd be a shining example of what's possible when you combine skill, passion, and a genuine desire to serve the customer.

The salesmen would function as a true team, united by common goals: satisfied customers and increased profits. They'd collaborate, share leads, assist one another in closing deals, and celebrate their collective success. And poor Shelley—the struggling salesman with a daughter in the hospital—he would enjoy robust health insurance to cover her care and a compassionate manager to accommodate his hospital visits.

When the motivational speaker from the front office appears, he wouldn't resort to threats and vulgarities. Instead, he'd fire up the team with meaningful ideas and shared values, encouraging them to build on their strengths. After all, they had made it this far—what had brought them success, and how could they leverage it to reach new heights?

And the customers? They would be content, perhaps even delighted, with their investments. Rather than feeling bullied or taken advantage of, they'd feel supported and valued. Some might even return for future investments or recommend the firm to friends and family. No more late-night cold calls or high-pressure tactics forcing hasty decisions with lasting consequences. Instead, referrals would flow naturally, a testament to the firm's integrity and reputation.

Of course, this happy scenario has a fatal flaw. While it sounds like a wonderful business model, it would make for a dreadful movie. The drama of the real film is in the intensity and raw emotion of its frantic characters, the ferocious competition, and the calamitous downfall. A kinder, gentler workplace like the one I described just wouldn't have the same visceral impact on the screen.

There's another defect in my happy workplace. It comes across as contrived and pie-in-the-sky even, which is the real tragedy. We can more readily accept the over-the-top viciousness of *Glengarry Glen Ross* than its opposite. Toxicity is expected, normal even. But why can't a more collaborative, respectful, and ethical workplace be the norm? The very fact that my reimagined version of *Glengarry Glen Ross*—call it *Glengarry Good Boss*—feels so unsatisfying and unrealistic is a testament to how far we still have to go.

I encourage you to watch the film less as a commentary on masculine corruption and more as a workplace drama—a critique of modern office culture. Great leadership committed to treating people as human beings, not just "resources" or "marks," would transform this sales office and likely boost sales in the end. It might not make the best cinema, but such a workplace replicated far and wide surely would be a welcome change in the world.

Section 3: The Sharper the Blade, the Safer the Knife

It seems counterintuitive, but a sharp knife is much safer than a dull one. If you've ever prepared food, you know what I mean.

It's the same with leadership. You must "sharpen the saw," as Stephen Covey famously advised in *The 7 Habits of Highly Effective People*. In that spirit, to be a great leader, you must be sharp.

Chapter 15: You Deserve to Be Disciplined

> "Teachers who do not take their own education seriously, who do not study, who make little effort to keep abreast of events have no moral authority to coordinate the activities of the classroom."
>
> —Paulo Freire, *Pedagogy of Freedom*

How well have you mastered the discipline of leadership? It's elementary that engineering majors study engineering to become engineers; history majors study history to become historians; biology majors study biology to become biologists. And English majors? They study English to become ... Englishmen.

(Pause for laughter.)

We call these areas of study "disciplines." By learning them, we can better understand each specialized field, and it's no different with leadership.

For many years, I had the honor of serving on the board of the American Conference of Academic Deans (ACAD). This national organization supports university deans and other academic executives. ACAD members devote themselves to the principle that—even though they're learned and accomplished in their individual scholarly fields, such as engineering, history, biology, or even English—they must now master a whole new discipline: leadership. Sadly, this perspective remains a minority view among deans outside of ACAD.

You've probably heard clichés like, "Leaders are born, not made," or "True leaders are forged in moments of crisis." While these sayings have a sliver of truth, the reality is far more nuanced. The vast majority of leaders—and every truly great leader—reach their potential by immersing themselves in the study and practice of leadership. (To be clear, I'm not talking about bosses here.)

As ACAD maintains, leadership is a discipline. If you want to excel at it, you must study it, practice what you learn, evaluate your practice, and refine your approach.

So, in the spirit of ACAD, let's examine what it takes to master the discipline of leadership, whatever your field.

Great Leaders Hit the Books (And Then Some)

As someone once said, "Leaders are readers." All great leaders are students of leadership. Study can come in a variety of forms, though. Reading is vital, but just carefully observing the performance of great leaders and the failures of poor leaders can be illuminating and often revelatory. To master leadership, you can attend leadership talks, watch leadership videos, listen to leadership podcasts, and sign up for courses. There's lots to learn and lots of ways to learn.

But beware of so-called experts (yes, including coaches and consultants like me) who try to sell you one-size-fits-all leadership models. Not that what they offer is necessarily wrong, but it's often misleadingly inadequate or impossibly complicated to implement.

The basics of leadership, though, are universal and serve as a foundation for great leadership:

1. **Human decency:** As I suggest in Chapter 1, just be decent. We're not just talking about being nice here. Decency is a skill to learn, hone, and use daily. You start with self-awareness, assess your values, and then live them. That's integrity. Need a shortcut to decency? Here it is: don't be a jerk. Simple.

2. **Ego wrangling:** We explore this idea in Chapter 3. Regularly and vigorously stuff that ego of yours in a sack and toss it in the river. Don't worry, it won't drown. But there's nothing quite like a soggy ego to keep you humble.

3. **Curiosity:** Nurture a spirit of ongoing inquiry—wondering, questioning, learning. We consider this idea in Chapter 12, and we'll do a deeper dive here.

I'm not saying that these three elements will magically transform you into a statue-worthy leader. After all, no matter how solid your foundation, it's useless without the house. At the same time, no matter how lovely the house, it'll collapse without a firm foundation.

And as with any discipline, the learning never stops. There's no finish line for the curious leader.

Great Leaders Dive Right In

Remember the old joke, "How do you get to Carnegie Hall?" Answer: "Practice, practice, practice!"

(Pause for laughter.)

Putting what you've learned into practice is not separate from the learning process—it's an essential part of it. The practice of leadership is simply a natural and necessary extension of learning leadership.

Here's a truth that bears repeating: perfection is a lie. If your goal is perfection, you're setting yourself up for failure. Great leaders understand that while striving for improvement is vital, the pursuit of perfection leads to inevitable frustration, disappointment, and failure. These are corrosive emotions—industrial-strength psychic solvents—that can erode the very foundation of your decency, humility, and willingness to learn.

Moreover, integrity is a cornerstone of great leadership. True leaders don't selectively practice their values; they live them consistently. Leadership isn't something you apply in one situation but ignore in another. The best leaders embody great leadership in everything they do, every day.

Great Leaders Take a Long, Hard Look in the Mirror

If you're an expert in anything, you know you must continually test and evaluate your skills to stay on top of your game. The same is true of mastering the discipline of leadership. Great leaders revisit their assumptions and assess their actions. They constantly question themselves:

- How sound is my understanding of leadership?
- Why do I lead the way I do?
- Do my actions match my values?
- What impact does my leadership have?
- What can I do to become a better leader?

They check with others, asking their team members, peers, and superiors the same questions.

Great Leaders Change Course

Now that you've reevaluated your leadership, it's time to act on what you've learned. Sometimes, this means applying your understanding and approach. Other times, it might mean chucking an outdated idea altogether because circumstances have changed or you were wrong. Great leaders own up to their mistakes, but that's not enough. They must also learn from them and act to prevent future errors.

Great Leaders Close the Loop

Have you noticed that this whole leadership development process is the same as how you learn anything? Grasping new material, putting it into practice, evaluating the results, and then revising. These revisions become your new understanding, and with that, you start all over again:

1. Learn something new.
2. Give it a go.
3. See how it went.
4. Make adjustments.
5. Repeat.

The learning process is iterative, a closed loop just like the discipline of leadership:

1. Learn.
2. Practice.
3. Evaluate.
4. Revise.
5. Close the loop.

To become a leader of integrity, you must be disciplined. Treat leadership like any other discipline or skill you want to acquire. Great leaders don't just lead; they master the art and science of leadership itself. Anything less is just flaccid bossing, which we have in abundance. No, the world desperately needs more great leaders, so get cracking!

Chapter 16: Soft Skills Are the Hardest Skills of All

"The future belongs to those who learn more skills and combine them in creative ways."

—Robert Greene

My first administrative position at a university was as the founding dean of the School of Humanities and Social Sciences. While my education and professional background were firmly rooted in the humanities, I quickly realized there was much to learn about the social sciences and their relationship to the humanities as I worked to unite two distinct academic areas (and 15 disciplines!) into one cohesive school.

You've certainly heard these terms—"humanities" and "social sciences"—but what do they mean? The humanities encompass disciplines such as philosophy, religion, English, and often history. Meanwhile, the social sciences include psychology, sociology, economics, political science, and sometimes history. (Yes, history is an interdisciplinary free agent!) In academia, I could name countless other fields with overlaps, underlaps, interlaps, meta-laps, and even burlaps—but you get the idea.

What might surprise those outside the academy is how territorial and fiercely competitive traditional liberal arts fields can be. Consider, for instance, the strained relationship captured in the oft-used terms "soft sciences" and "hard sciences." The behavioral and social sciences are labeled "soft" (read: *inadequate, simplistic,* or *less rigorous*), while the natural sciences are deemed "hard" (read: *robust, challenging,* and *consequential*).

As strange as such hierarchies may seem to those outside academia, there's more. The humanities are dismissed as not serious (read: *mushy*). Lower still in the pecking order, the fine and performing arts are categorized as softer still (read: *squishy*). These examples illustrate the disciplinary caste system that plagues academia and shapes societal perceptions.

Yet despite these distinctions and hierarchies, significant commonalities exist among these fields. For example, the natural sciences and social sciences share research methodologies and some terminology. At the same time, while humanistic methodologies are often more fluid than those of the natural and social sciences, the humanities and social sciences intersect in their pursuit of fundamental questions and inferences about the human experience.

Ironically, academic humanists themselves sometimes regard the fine and performing arts as insufficiently serious or scholarly, even as they draw heavily from them for their content, methods of understanding, and broader insights.

For those keeping score, then, the traditional and entirely unreasonable pecking order of liberal arts disciplines is:

1. Natural sciences (hard)
2. Social sciences (soft)
3. Humanities (mushy)
4. Arts (squishy)

To be sure, competent academic professionals eschew this silly disciplinary sorting, which is largely the obsession of the arrogant and the ignorant. Solid academic professionals readily bridge the gaps between fields, capitalize on their similarities and synergies, and exploit their differences to collaborate on better-serving students and scholarship.

What Are Soft Skills?

Just as some dismiss the social sciences as soft, employers sometimes dismiss the arts, social sciences, and humanities as basic training in mere soft skills. There's a pronounced pliability at play in these fields that's allegedly not so important to other fields, such as the natural sciences or business.

Soft skills, though, are deemed soft because they demand mastery of human nature's plasticity—or softness—while hard skills help us perform particular tasks in a specific field. For example, the ability to persuade constitutes a soft skill in the workplace, while the ability to utilize a database is a hard skill. Both skills can be learned, but soft skills resist easy measurement. Meanwhile, hard skills are often more readily quantified.

Importantly, despite the negative implications of the term "soft skills," when employers are surveyed about what abilities they most value when hiring, the response invariably focuses on communication, critical thinking, leadership, teamwork, problem-solving, creativity, and so on. In other words, the very soft skills they denigrate.

Note that all these soft skills defy easy definition but are transferable across most, if not all, professional fields. Physicians and lawyers generally need them just as much as elementary school teachers and theater actors.

What Are Human Skills?

I prefer to think of "soft skills" as "human skills," but I'm not going to list them here. If you want lists—you can easily Google phrases like "The 7 Soft Skills," "The Top 10 Soft Skills," or "50 Examples of Soft Skills." You'll get more than you bargained for.

But here's the catch: effectively utilizing these human skills—the ones most critical for thriving in human-centered contexts—is far from simple. Mastery requires deep contemplation, thoughtful analysis, and continuous practice. Often, the journey begins with a healthy dose of demystification.

Those who cultivate a comprehensive array of these skills tend to stand out. They elevate themselves beyond mere competence to extraordinary achievement, distinguishing themselves among their peers. Not coincidentally, these individuals also make the most successful and trusted leaders.

Such leaders inspire confidence and foster productivity. They rarely need to demand anything because their teams are intrinsically motivated to align with the leader's vision. They never use manipulation, coercion, or even basic reward systems like carrots and sticks. Instead, great leaders leverage human skills to get people to want to do what needs to be done.

Maintaining proficiency in these skills requires rigorous development, improvement, and refinement. And therein lies the paradox: these so-called "soft" skills are incredibly challenging to master and apply consistently, much more so than most so-called hard skills.

That's why soft skills—despite their moniker—are the hardest skills of all.

Chapter 17: The 4 Cs of Leadership Success

"I suppose leadership at one time meant muscles; but today it means getting along with people."

—Mahatma Gandhi

All great leaders rely on four essential elements to drive their success. As it happens, each of these fundamentals starts with the letter 'C.' Let's dive into these "4 Cs" of leadership success and explore how one builds on the other to shape effective leadership.

Character: The Foundation of Leadership

By character, I don't mean a character in a story, nor is it a euphemism for a quirky personality: "My goodness, she certainly is a real character, bless her heart!" Character, as I mean it, forms the foundation of leadership. It's who you are—your integrity, personality, experience, and values. Your behavior offers the best and most important reflection of your character, even if we all stumble from time to time.

I've been a supervisor, and I've had to let people go. The last time I did so, I blew it—a real failure of character. To be clear, this person had to go. She was a favorite of my predecessor, but her sense of entitlement made her as toxic as Chernobyl.

I gave her a full year to get it together, but her open hostility, rank insubordination, and seemingly willful incompetence left me with no options. Want a sample of how bad it was? After she left, we discovered voodoo dolls of her co-workers hidden throughout her office. Strategically placed pins impaled their little bodies. Ouch!

I could've handled the whole episode better, but my worst failure of character came on the day I fired her. I was only one year into my position, and I caved to my mean-spirited boss's preferred termination method. Her technique required HR to hand the employee a one-sentence dismissal notice, refuse to answer questions, and then have security escort them out. Have a nice weekend!

As a supervisor, I was supposed to be absent, but I insisted on at least being in HR when the employee came in. Then, I obediently left the building as the deed was done. To this day, I cringe thinking about how she must have felt, treated like a failed piece of equipment as security escorted her off the premises. Had I tapped into my integrity, had I acted as a leader, I would have defied my cruel boss and granted this woman a modicum of human decency by being present in that moment, instead of dumping her off to her fate.

Even knowing how truly appalling this employee was, I'm most appalled at my failure of character. In that situation, I was no leader at all.

Communication: The Lifeblood of Leadership

Communication is the lifeblood that nourishes relationships, and relationships are the pumping heart of effective leadership. Great communication is a two-way street, and exceptional leaders build relationships by listening first.

Early in my years as a senior supervisor, I inherited some challenging employees. One in particular was extremely confrontational and unreasonable. When I had to tell him that a committee had denied a request he had made, I botched it spectacularly.

Frankly, I just wanted to be done with the ugly business and with him, so I didn't consider how badly the news would affect him. My message to him came across as dismissively curt, one-sided, and inconsiderate. It further damaged our already tenuous relationship, which I never succeeded in repairing despite years of effort on my part. Boy, that guy could hold a grudge!

Like the employee in my first example, this guy was incorrigible, but I can't help wondering if we could have achieved even a smidgen of collegiality had I taken the time to communicate with him properly from the start.

You see, for communication to have any value or effectiveness, it needs to be values-based—a matter of having solid character. On this occasion, I flunked the test of character; therefore, my communication and leadership suffered.

Compromise: The Key to Progress

Compromise sometimes gets a bad rap, but it's crucial for getting things done as a leader. Still, people resist altering their expectations because they view compromise as a failure. Think about how we use the word in phrases: "a compromised reputation," "a compromised immune system," or "a compromised machine part."

In leadership, though, compromise is the magic potion that gives rise to the politics of possibility. It's how we move things forward when working with others. Strangely, we often think refusing to budge even a little is the high mark of integrity, but that's rarely the case.

As a university dean, I had a boss who would take outlandish and indefensible stances. Once, he publicly and angrily rejected a course proposal by one of my academic departments. His reasoning wasn't just flawed; he actually accused the faculty of highly unethical intentions. His behavior was bizarrely over the top, even for him.

In reality, the course proposal simply updated an existing course to align it with current standards in the field. But my boss would have none of this. He opposed the course, and that was that. Instead of seeking compromise, I joined him in unreason by digging in my heels. I decided this dispute was a hill to die on, and I nearly did.

Eventually, he backed down, but our disagreement dragged on for weeks across the holiday season and into the following semester. He was furious with me. The good news was that I prevented him from violating the faculty's academic freedom and protected them and the curriculum. But what might a small compromise on my part have accomplished?

Compromise means that all parties give up something. It could be a little or a lot. Indeed, one party might concede much more than another, but both must contribute something for it to be a true compromise. The give-and-take of compromise—its transactional nature—demands clear communication as well as solid character since true compromise revolves around trust.

Although my boss had publicly backed himself into a position and didn't want to lose face, I offered him no out. It was all or nothing. If I had acted as a leader then, I would have recognized his predicament and offered him a small concession—maybe revising some of the language in the proposal. I could have provided him cover by giving just a little. Instead, I treated the dispute as a game I had to win at all costs. It could have gone even worse than it did, but our fragile relationship had shattered nonetheless.

Collaboration: The Ultimate Leadership Goal

Competition often gets undue credit for driving innovation and progress. In truth, collaboration is the most powerful tool in a leader's kit. Competition has a flaw: it operates on zero-sum logic. There must be winners, and there must be losers. As one person surges, another falls behind.

Collaboration, on the other hand, creates win-win scenarios by pooling resources and ideas to achieve levels of success no single entity could reach alone—more than the sum of its parts. Building a culture of collaboration is the leader's ultimate endeavor.

Let me share a more positive example from my time as a dean. My faculty regularly offered intriguing elective courses that I didn't feel were getting the attention they deserved. So, we started putting together and printing lists each semester of what we called "Cool Courses" to highlight these gems. We chose print over digital so it would feel more novel to the students and produced unique (and very silly) covers to catch the eye. The campaign was successful, with people looking forward to seeing our latest list every term.

One of my fellow deans had a competitive streak, and one semester she produced a rival catalog for her school called "Hot Courses." I admit it was a clever and funny send-up of my efforts. She was an artist, and her covers were the more polished version of what I was trying to pull off.

The contest started out friendly enough, but having two competing catalogs confused students and diluted our efforts. We soon realized we'd be better off joining forces. We agreed to continue producing our own separate course lists, but we bound them together back-to-back and upside down. That way, whichever way you looked at it, one of our course lists was always on top.

We continued our friendly competition for the most striking cover (which she always won), but we also extended our reach to students and boosted our course enrollments together. Our competition had evolved into a true collaboration that benefited both our schools and all our students. We had been good on our own, and now we were even better together.

To achieve true collaboration, you start with a spirit of compromise. My fellow dean and I both sacrificed a great deal of independence to coordinate our joint venture. Doing so also required clear communication and mutual trust, which only solid character can establish.

* * *

So as you can see, the 4 Cs of leadership form a progression. It starts with character, which lays the groundwork for communication. Character-based communication, in turn, makes compromise possible, and honest compromise fosters collaboration:

1. Character

2. Communication
3. Compromise
4. Collaboration

While securing some accomplishments as a leader without all four qualities may be possible, your chances of ongoing success soar when you embrace all four. Mastering and applying the 4 Cs of leadership—character, communication, compromise, and collaboration—will ensure you're on the path to true and lasting leadership.

Chapter 18: The 3 Keys to Unlocking Effective Communication

"You want to talk to me,
Go ahead and talk."

—Bob Dylan, "Tight Connection to My Heart
(Has Anyone Seen My Love)"

As I note in Chapter 17, communication is the second of the four elements of leadership success—the 4 Cs: character, communication, compromise, and collaboration. Moreover, communication underpins every successful human interaction and organization, regardless of size or type. Written and oral communication serves as our primary conduit for directives, ideas, and inspiration and allows us to foster an environment of productivity, cohesion, and growth. Conversely, a lack of effective communication renders every interaction and organization dysfunctional.

All impactful communication consists of three interwoven and equally vital components—three keys to unlock effective communication:

- A valuable message
- A known and receptive audience
- Impeccable clarity

The Power of a Valuable Message

The first key is a *valuable message*. It isn't enough to have something to say; what you say must have significance and be worth saying. The most potent messages are firmly rooted in understandable and relatable values.

Consider the classic fable "The Boy Who Cried Wolf." You know the tale. A boy, tasked with watching over sheep, decides to play a prank by falsely alerting the townsfolk that a wolf is attacking their flock. Because he's lying, his message lacks value, and he instantly demonstrates his untrustworthiness. The consequences are dire: no one believes the young shepherd's cries when an actual wolf attacks and devours the sheep (and the boy). This tale vividly illustrates the critical importance of values in delivering meaningful messages.

The fable applies to the working world as well. Supervisors' messages typically fall into two categories: *informational* and *inspirational*. While informational messages, like the shepherd boy's cries, may not always explicitly reflect good values, they must be built upon solid principles, such as honesty.

Consider your own experiences. How often have you rolled your eyes at an email from your boss or skimmed through verbose communications that seemed to convey only a single message: a lack of respect for your time? Alternately, have you ever worked under a boss so demanding or duplicitous that you scrutinized every missive as if it were holy scripture, rife with hidden meanings and traps? Perhaps you preserved them, printing them out and archiving them "to have a record."

In either scenario, you're dealing with a boss whose values are suspect and, subsequently, whose messages hold little worth beyond the fact that your contemptible boss sent them. By generating confusion, fear, and paranoia—the enemies of productivity—such communications merely distract you from the your actual work.

The same is true of inspirational messages. They must originate in and express positive values to be effective. Take, for example, a university president I knew who gave frequent speeches to his staff about good leadership and teamwork. While the content of the speeches was sensible (having been written by his aide), the president's typically despicable behavior sapped their value.

Even as he delivered his lofty lectures, he violated their underlying principles by treating his underlings condescendingly and lording his position over them. The glaring hypocrisy often proved excruciating for his captive audience, causing his otherwise sound messages to fall flat and eliciting audible scoffs from listeners.

The Importance of a Known and Receptive Audience

The second key to communication is a *known* and *receptive audience.* While having a valuable message is crucial, understanding who will receive it is equally important; otherwise, you'll struggle to connect. Moreover, your audience must be open to hearing your message. In short, you have to be willing to learn from and be sensitive to your audience before they can hear from and be sensitive to you and your message.

Let's revisit "The Boy Who Cried Wolf," but with a twist. Imagine the shepherd boy was honest, but the townsfolk were less reliable. Let's say that—unbeknownst to him—they had insured their flock for an exorbitant amount and were more interested in the potential payout than the well-being of their sheep. How might they, as the audience, respond to the boy's authentic cries for help when the wolf threatened?

The university president I mentioned often invited industry leaders from outside higher education to address top administrators. For whatever reason, most of those experts mistakenly assumed they were speaking to faculty, which wasn't the case. This disconnect between the presumed and actual audiences invariably resulted in the speakers' failure to communicate their intended message effectively, no matter how powerful that message happened to be. The administrators simply didn't want to hear it.

Furthermore, receptivity is pivotal even if the audience is correctly identified. For instance, consider a scenario where those same experts were indeed addressing the faculty but chose to lecture about teaching methods. The faculty would certainly take offense since none of the speakers were educators. Even if the lecture content were perfectly sound, professors would struggle to sit quietly while being professionally slighted by a presumptuous speaker. Tailoring a message to be heard most effectively by your audience is often a matter of rhetoric—the art of persuasion.

When considering your audience, remember this truth: *in communication, the audience has all the power*. I describe this phenomenon—the "messaging paradox"—in Chapter 26. In short, your audience is free to hear you, ignore you, or interpret your words in ways entirely different from your intention, and you're powerless to control the outcome. Indeed, the ear proves mightier than the mouth!

The Necessity of Impeccable Clarity

The third indispensable key to effective communication is *impeccable clarity*. Let's say you have an important, values-based message and an audience primed to hear it. Unfortunately, if your delivery is unclear, no one will understand your intended meaning, rendering your message meaningless.

The essence of communication lies not in verbosity or complexity but in *lucidity*—ensuring that the message transmits seamlessly from sender to receiver. Would you address a group of English speakers exclusively in German? Would you speak to civil engineers using medical jargon? As absurd as those questions seem, I'm sure you can find plenty of equally absurd examples in your own experience: the politician who speaks in word salads, the memo that buries its point in paragraphs of meaningless fluff, or the instructions so poorly written or translated that you can't make heads or tails of them.

Clarity is, in part, a function of knowing your audience since it can differ from listener to listener. Just as addressing English speakers in another language would render your message meaningless, you need to tailor your style to your audience and circumstances to ensure it resonates. Otherwise, what's the point? Even the best message, when poorly or improperly delivered, fails to achieve its purpose.

Let's return to "The Boy Who Cried Wolf" one final time, but now the shepherd boy is the most trustworthy of characters, and the townsfolk are eager to protect their flock. This time, though, when the wolf arrives, instead of just yelling, "Wolf," this pompous little boy cries out, "There appears to be a large predatory canid of ferocious countenance on the prowl!" The simple townsfolk might hear this and assume the boy's gone a bit batty from being alone on the hill. They reluctantly send one person to investigate, but by then it's too late.

Simply put, *clarity trumps everything*, meaning you must do whatever it takes to be as clear as possible. Even the rules of grammar become secondary to the imperative for clarity.

Years ago, when I founded a school as a new dean at my university, I faced a pressing challenge. I needed to foster cooperation and collaboration among the 15 disciplines comprising the new school. To accomplish this, I established representative working groups to develop our foundational documents and headed the committee for drafting the new school's statement of purpose myself.

From the outset, the group was highly collegial, and we all agreed that our statement would serve as the core of our fledgling culture. Despite all that goodwill, we struggled with the language of the statement—after all, we were academics—and clarity eluded us. Our main sticking point was that each discipline preferred its own specialized vocabulary—its jargon.

Once we recognized this disconnect, we could see our way forward. We abandoned jargon to build a common language around shared values, which is the essence of a statement of purpose. That common language clearly articulated our message and values, allowing the statement to resonate with our faculty, students, and the general public. Long after I left that university, the statement remained in use.

A valuable message, a known and receptive audience, and unwavering clarity: these are the three keys to effective communication. The more robust each element, the more impactful your communication. Great leaders recognize that communication is the lifeblood of organizational success, so they prioritize all three to lead their teams to continued progress. Simply put, if you want to be a great leader, you must become a great communicator by mastering the three keys.

Chapter 19: Every Leadership Challenge Is a Teaching Challenge

"Teachers touch eternity through their students."

—Freeman Hrabowski

Every leadership challenge is a teaching challenge. In other words, the same skills you'd use to teach are precisely the ones an effective leader needs. Now, when I talk about teaching, I'm drawing on my background as a college professor and administrator. But please, don't conjure a sepia-toned image of some tweed-clad egghead perched on a platform behind a podium, droning on as students attempt to capture his (yes, *his*) pearls of wisdom in their notepads.

That outdated model is rightly derided as the "sage on the stage" mode of lecturing. It and its variants may work for a few students—the very special few who could still learn if you locked them in a windowless room with only a book and a lamp. For the rest of humanity, the most effective instructors rely on dynamic interaction rather than lectures.

But this is an essay about leadership, not teaching, or—more precisely—it's about the intersection of effective teaching and effective leadership. To be clear, the sorts of problems that beset leaders in almost any field are just variations of the problems teachers face in class. They may differ in particulars, scope, and stakes, but—and this is important—the ways of coping are re-markably similar.

In no particular order, here are a few (not all) necessities for being an effective college teacher and how they pertain to leadership.

1. Teachers and leaders set goals.

Good teachers need good goals. I'm not talking about metrics like grades. Good teachers know where they're directing their students and what they want them to take away from the experience. Yes, there are assignments and tests, but a superior teacher understands that those are mostly crude instruments for assessing what a student has learned.

The true objective is the learning itself. And challenging goals motivate better than insipid ones. Moreover, rigorous goals achieve more than merely difficult ones. There's a stark difference between rigor and rigmarole.

The same for leaders. You want your people to complete their tasks and behave in certain ways—in other words, do their jobs with little fuss. But what do you ultimately want from them or, more compellingly, for them? Remember, it may not be easily gauged or measured at all. The good news is that the measure is less important than the achievement.

2. Teachers and leaders plan carefully.

Related to goal setting is planning, and the first rule of planning is "know thy stuff."

In grad school, I had a fabulous professor named Linda Hutcheon. She told this horrifying/hilarious story about the first time she had to give a lecture. She was extremely busy and never got around to reading the novel she was supposed to teach, *Great Expectations* by Charles Dickens, which, as they say, is a bear. She found herself behind a podium with a room full of impatient students and an hour to fill, so she proceeded to give an entire lesson on just the book's first paragraph.

Linda is brilliant and charismatic, so she could pull off such a stunt. I certainly couldn't. But while she was no doubt engaging and even remarkably insightful, the lecture was probably not particularly enlightening for the students. She knew her stuff in that she knew how to belabor the reading of a single paragraph, but she didn't know the novel as a whole and could offer nothing of worth on that score.

Once you fully know your stuff, though, there are two things to consider in planning. First, there's the opposite of what Linda did: overplanning, laying everything out minutely. You've heard the proverb, "The best-laid schemes of mice and men often go awry." The line is adapted from the Scottish poet Robert Burns and warns against expecting plans to turn out just so.

The second is sticking to the plan no matter what. When I first started teaching, I was advised to have a lesson plan broken down into ten-minute increments, and I stupidly heeded this advice with predictable results. Instead of focusing on the students, their needs, their pacing, and their learning, I focused on staying on track. It's the same with bosses who are more concerned with time-on-task, progress reports, and arbitrary deadlines than getting things done.

One of the paradoxes of planning is that the more thorough the planning, the more freedom you have to adapt or abandon your plan as needed. My best classes were where I threw out my lesson plan and winged it. I had great semesters when, fifteen minutes into just about every class, I'd dramatically crumple my lesson plan into a ball and toss it into a trash can. The students would howl delightedly because they knew we were off the races. And here's the thing. Although we got there via an unexpected route, by the end of the semester, we always covered all the necessary material while assuring that the students were truly engaged in learning it.

How could I do this? My careful preparation gave me the understanding and confidence to try something different in the moment, to explode the status quo when needed.

Great leaders know how, when, and why and are willing—even enthusiastic—to explode the status quo to get better results. Mere bosses stick to their guns come hell or high water.

3. Teachers and leaders communicate effectively.

This one should be a no-brainer, but it escapes so many leaders. Good teachers make it their mission to communicate clearly with their students, but they're equally keen to listen to their students—not just what they say but also the nuances and inflections of how they say it. Most of the communication from students, by the way, is non-verbal. Good teachers can tell when students have something on their minds but remain silent. Really good teachers can do so on Zoom.

Communication is about conversation. How did I know when to abandon a lesson plan? Because my students told me when. To be clear, they never said, "Hey, Dr. Sal, why don't you throw away that lesson plan." They told me through their responses to the material—their answers, the questions they asked, and their unspoken reactions or non-reactions, including utter silence. In short, we had conversations, even when I was doing most of or all the talking. I was open to them, which allowed them to open up to me and each other.

As I maintain in Chapter 18, when it comes to communication, clarity trumps everything.

How does this teaching practice differ from effective leadership? Not one jot.

4. Teachers and leaders guide.

Computer scientist and economist Herbert A. Simon once observed, "The teacher can advance learning only by influencing what the student does to learn." In other words, teachers guide, just as leaders do.

To my claim that "every leadership challenge is a teaching challenge," I sometimes add, "and every teaching challenge is a teaching-of-composition challenge." Those who have taught college composition or another rigorous skill-based course know exactly what I mean.

You can provide people with information and guide them toward understanding and practice, but they must fully engage in learning on their own. My friend and colleague Jerry Van Aken summed it up this way: "You can lead a student to knowledge, but you can't make them think." Quite.

Same for leaders. Some processes consist only of rote steps—like IKEA instructions. But if a process involves any degree of comprehension, a leader can only guide people to fully grasp what's needed. This is even more true when the process requires interpretation, evaluation, or adaptation. Therefore, good leaders take on the role of attentive guide.

Meanwhile, the worst bosses are the ones who constantly say, "I have to do everything myself because everyone else is incompetent." Can you guess who is the real incompetent in that scenario? It's the same with teachers who complain about their students being too "stupid" to learn. Can you guess who is the real fool in that classroom?

I'll go one step further. A truly great leader invites others to explore ideas and systems, guiding them, breaking things down step-by-step, and walking with them through the process. Leadership expert and psychologist John Amaechi argues that great leaders should engage others in a way that says, "Not only does your path to success exist, but I'm going to walk it with you." That's literally how great teachers approach their craft.

Such a leader allows people to reach their goals in their own way as much as possible. You can often tell an organization that has a lot of bosses but no true leadership by the number of rigid or bureaucratic rules and procedures in place. Yes, some are essential, especially in certain contexts, but when they exist or are enforced arbitrarily—for their own sake—they stifle true leadership. Productivity suffers.

Here are a few other areas where good teaching and leadership overlap:

- Patient repetition
- Breaking large, complex tasks into manageable steps
- Cutting some slack
- Not being a jerk
- Following through
- Focusing on equity and fairness

There are many more, of course. The point is that great leaders are, in fact, great teachers (and vice versa), and engaged followers are like students eager to grow and succeed. The more you understand these truths and intentionally adopt the mindset of an effective teacher the better you can lead.

Chapter 20: Occam's Razor, the Invaluable Miracle Tool You Can't Live Without

"Beauty walks a razor's edge, someday
I'll make it mine."

—Bob Dylan, "Shelter from the Storm"

Here's a quick quiz. You're at the baseball stadium watching your favorite team. The game is entering the ninth inning, and your team's starting pitcher has given up no hits and no walks. Not a single opponent has been on base. There's a buzz in the air, a strained hush combined with a tense murmur. People are furtively pointing toward the scoreboard in excitement and holding up their phones to take photo after photo of every pitch. Meanwhile, you're dismayed that although his pitch count is low, the pitcher looks gassed, and his speed and accuracy are dropping.

You've been keeping an eye on the guy sitting next to you—some rube wearing a tee-shirt with an image of the opposing team's mascot and sporting a trucker's hat with the Cabella's logo. He's on his fourth ballpark Chardonnay, which might be what prompts him to gush loudly to the woman next to him, "Gee, honey. we might get to see a perfect game! Too bad it's the other team."

You instantly wince along with every fan within earshot. Sure enough, the next batter up, the visiting team's best slugger launches one over the centerfield fence. You seethe with rage. So much for the perfect game! So much for the no-hitter! So much for the shut-out!

What do you conclude?

A. The rube sitting next to you has jinxed your pitcher by speaking aloud of the potential perfect game, a baseball taboo.

B. The pitcher colluded with local bookies to run up the betting action before purposely blowing the no-hitter in the ninth inning.

C. The pitcher was clearly physically and mentally fatigued and facing a formidable batter under a great deal of stress, so the home run should be no surprise.

As much as the acolytes and guardians of baseball superstition may want the answer to be A, and as much as cynical conspiracy theorists and out-of-luck gamblers want it to be B, logic dictates that the answer is C. But how do we know? After all, even if you're not superstitious, isn't it within the realm of possibility that there's such a thing in this universe as jinxing? Can you prove there's no such thing? By the same reasoning, can you prove there was no gambling conspiracy?

The fact is that it's impossible to prove a negative to an absolute, which is why most functioning justice systems worldwide put the burden of proof on prosecutors. The possibility of a jinx, criminal conspiracy, extraterrestrial influence, a magic whammy executed by the opposing team's official sorcerer, or any number of reasons you can imagine all remain in the category of the possible so long as someone believes they do. Possible, though, it is categorically different from probable or even serious.

Simply put, because you can conceive such scenarios, they're, by definition, not inconceivable, however illogical. After all, the human mind is a meaning-making machine, well-oiled by a lubricious (in every sense) imagination, and our ability to speculate is, frankly, awesome.

Every day and in many situations, we face the dilemma of determining what's most likely true and what's merely possible on an infinitely diminishing scale. Whether large or small, distant or local, we must make sense of these dilemmas to successfully navigate our world. A disciplined, rational mind can do so with relative aplomb.

Admittedly, rationality does not yield perfection, but it does operate with a high degree of accuracy, much more so than irrational imaginings or mere guesses. That's why—even though they're often wrong—we still consult meteorologists when planning a day at the beach rather than relying on Aunt Gladys's trusty rheumatic flare-ups.

Enlightening the Rational

Without getting too political, I challenge you to consider our present day. There's probably some well-established fact you hold near and dear that faces persistent challenges to its veracity. The challenges may even morph as they are debunked, always with the assumption that each new manifestation must be real because it's imaginable.

Despite our supposedly rational nature, vast swaths of the population regularly practice "appeals to ignorance" to deny verified facts and defy basic logic. This indulgence leads to wild conclusions with profound and dangerous consequences for individuals and society. It also renders the overly credulous ripe for manipulation. Be they election truthers, flat-Earthers, Holocaust deniers, climate-change skeptics, or Qanon, the ascendancy and sway of nonsensical and often self-contradictory theories have led some to speculate that we're reaching the limit of the Enlightenment's influence.

The Enlightenment, or Age of Reason, was an eighteenth-century epistemological shift in European thinking. It arguably helped dissolve Europe's adherence to superstition and magical thinking, ushering in a new era marked by the primacy of logic and the scientific method. It also birthed the philosophy behind the founding of the United States.

That period's movement away from Medieval metaphysics has allowed our society to enjoy a long—though inequitable and imperfect—period of ascendant rationality, decent medical treatment, and stellar sanitation. If that rational era is coming to a close, how can we dependably cut through rising irrational speculation and unwarranted belief to get to the heart of truth? To do so, we'd need a pretty sharp implement, something like a razor.

Which brings us to good old Occam.

Well before the Enlightenment, William of Ockham—commonly Occam—a fourteenth-century English friar and philosopher, formulated a beautifully elegant heuristic known as "Occam's Razor." Often, we render it as something like, "When faced with a problem, the simplest answer is usually the correct one." This formulation is a bit misleading but good enough for most daily situations.

In actuality, Occam merely suggested that in solving problems, we shouldn't add anything not already in evidence. That way, we can keep idle speculation to a minimum. In other words, try to solve problems and dilemmas using only available evidence. Don't introduce anything, and certainly don't make things up.

So let's apply Occam's razor to the case of our disappointed baseball pitcher. We have no documentation of a nefarious gambling scheme. Nor is there any reasonable proof of a wondrous cosmic influence that bizarrely and confoundingly seems entirely localized on baseball diamonds (aka the "jinx"). Therefore, Occam's razor dictates that—given the available evidence—the pitcher's visible exhaustion in the face of a tough opponent likely caused him to blow his perfect game.

It's important to understand that Occam's razor isn't an absolute and was never intended to be. For instance, when analyzing a problem, there may exist evidence that you're unaware of when you deploy the razor. Maybe some gambling cabal you just haven't heard about influenced the outcome. Therefore, try to be thorough in your search for evidence and keep an open mind when applying Occam. Nonetheless, never concoct evidence.

Moreover, don't let the desire to reach a certain conclusion via confirmation bias or motivated reasoning cause you to ignore extenuating or contradictory evidence. When used properly, Occam's razor can slice such nonobjectivity to shreds.

Occam's razor remains an indispensable tool for drawing conclusions, solving problems, and resolving dilemmas. It's based on the simple principle that what you see is typically what you get—that the available evidence is usually sufficient to guide your reasoning to its conclusion and reveal the truth of a matter.

When wielded wisely, Occam's razor helps cut through poor reasoning and avoid wild or unfounded beliefs. It can trim away prejudice and groupthink. This tool is as useful for everyday problems as it is for tackling complex global issues. It can debunk lies, superstition, conspiracy theories, urban legends, and standard BS.

As impressive as that may sound, it's important to remember— it's not magic. In the end, it's just a razor.

Chapter 21: Introducing the Perception-Reality Razor

"Reality is based on your perception of the truth."

—Steven Aitchison

Leaders at every level need to understand this fundamental truth: an individual's perception is their reality. To clarify, I don't endorse the misguided idea that "everything I believe is true," nor do I sanction your right to force everyone to adopt your perception. In fact, confusion over this concept—or, more cynically, its active manipulation—has contributed to pushing this nation and world to the brink.

Wise leaders, however, recognize and respect that their people's perceptions are their reality. This principle becomes indispensable when crossing cultural divides, including but not limited to race, gender, sexual orientation, belief systems, class, and even organizational hierarchy.

Consider a scenario where a Black female employee tells her White male boss about experiencing workplace discrimination. Unless the boss has personally witnessed the discrimination, he has no direct access to her experiences, let alone her perceptions. In such a case, it's his responsibility to listen carefully and defer to her perspective unless evidence proves otherwise. This deference is also necessary if he has witnessed the discrimination himself but doesn't view it as significant.

While it may seem obvious that others experience events and realities differently from us, this idea is often difficult to grasp. It's human nature to reject unfamiliar perspectives, and some people even respond with irrational hostility to the very notion.

However, since we can never fully walk in someone else's proverbial shoes, it's wise to initially accept their perception as their reality. This doesn't mean adopting their perspective as your own but rather giving their perception space to exist while tempering your own assumptions accordingly.

Authorities often rush to constrain others' perceptions and impose their own, especially when those views challenge, discomfit, or inconvenience them. But it's important to remind ourselves that our reality is shaped by the quirks of our own perception. We see what we see and know what we know—real or not. Everything else, including how we interpret it, is conjecture.

How is one to cope with all these different perspectives and perceptions? I'm proposing the perception-reality razor—a heuristic tool for addressing problems and making people-based decisions. Like all razors—such as Occam's razor—it's a great tool to start with, but don't make it your only or even last tool.

Here's the longhand version of the perception-reality razor: *Always assume that another's perception is valid unless and until evidence or logic demonstrates otherwise.*

The shorthand version?
Perception is reality.

While most leaders wisely accept that a team member's perception—sometimes articulated as a complaint or criticism—is valid, exceptions will crop up. For instance, your past observations of this particular someone might justifiably lead you to quickly conclude the opposite. Let's say that person has proven time and again to be unreliable; then assuming this time is different may be foolhardy. But again, such situations are exceptions.

Furthermore, even—or particularly—when the person expresses concerns about the leader, the razor applies. Approaching others with empathy and openness almost always trumps the opposite tack and solves many problems before they can fester and grow.

And it's not only about complaints and accusations. Great leaders recognize that their team members' varied perspectives and perceptions can add to an organization's collective wisdom. Leaders don't have a monopoly on ideas and insight.

Mastering the perception-reality razor requires a leap of faith and often puts us at odds with our own perceptions and assumptions. Therefore, wielding the razor demands humility and resilience.

Finally, because it is all about human perceptions, the razor applies to the full range of human behaviors, including irrationality and dishonesty. In short, it's not easy to use, but compared to the folly of dismissing or disrespecting people's perceptions, applying the perception-reality razor is a pretty minor exertion.

Remember, as a heuristic tool, the perception-reality razor—that perception is reality—can clarify a situation quickly, but it's only a starting point. Use it wisely, and you'll find it another invaluable addition to your leadership toolkit.

Section 4: Learn to Duck the Dangers of Little Learning

Alexander Pope wrote, "A little learning is a dangerous thing." Leaders understand this notion on an intuitive level.

It's not enough to be sharp as a leader. You must ensure that you're not fooling yourself along the way.

Chapter 22: Want to Lead Better? Behave like an Iconoclast

"The eyes of the idol with the iron head are glowing."

—Bob Dylan, "Jokerman"

What is an iconoclast, and why should you, as a leader, behave like one? Most people have little memory of their graduation ceremonies: who spoke, what they said. Do you remember your graduation speaker? Do you remember the speech? Decades after graduation, I still strongly remember our keynote speaker, the evolutionary biologist Stephen Jay Gould. Over my many years working in higher education, I've heard a lot of graduation addresses, and Gould's was one of the best because he did what all the best ones do.

There are three main categories of graduation speakers. Some speakers primarily give advice based on their experience, which—though well-intentioned—like perspiration, evaporates soon after the nylon graduation gowns come off. Others focus on their personal saga of persisting through struggle and woe. Everyone applauds fervently, many cry, and most feel uplifted and inspired for a few hours before the memory fades into the background. These overcoming-adversity speeches are everyone's favorite, but they're the oratorical equivalent of cotton candy: colorful, intriguing, pleasing, insubstantial, and easily dissolved. Beware mental cavities.

Gould fell into the third and best speaker category, the one who knows their audience well and throws down a serious challenge to the graduates. My alma mater—Bard College—has long been known for its unconventional students, and he leaned into that reputation before giving us a charge to live the promise of our unorthodox ideals. He pointedly used a particular word to describe us, the same word several previous speakers that day had also used: "iconoclast."

So, what is an iconoclast?

If you look up the word "iconoclasm," you'll see something about people smashing religious icons, but that's a bit obscure and hopelessly literal. Merriam-Webster describes an iconoclast as "a person who attacks settled beliefs or institutions," which is true, but the word "attacks" seems a tad over the top and very limiting.

Really, an iconoclast, as we most often use the term today, is someone who isn't beholden to conventions and who questions cultural assumptions. Some people conflate the term with "skeptic," but a skeptic is more a thinker while an iconoclast is more a doer.

Great artists tend to be iconoclasts. For instance, you won't be surprised to learn that I'm a huge Bob Dylan fan. One of the things that attracts me to him is his artistic iconoclasm—this even though he himself is an icon. He breaks the rules so successfully that his innovations often become the new rule, which he then breaks. Nothing is sacred to the iconoclast.

Iconoclasm in Practice

Sitting not far from me during that graduation ceremony was my good friend Geoff. We have stayed tight since college and even pursued similar careers teaching English—he in high school and me in universities. A few years back, I had the privilege of spending a day in his public high school classroom in Philadelphia.

One of the things about teaching high school vs teaching college is the rigidity—what with secondary ed's standardized tests, standardized curricula, and standardized periods that terminate with a standardized buzzer. As hidebound bureaucratic relics, many of those standardized measures compete with the stated educational goals of the district. This conflict is a fine example of Goodhart's law at work—"When a measure becomes a target, it ceases to be a good measure"—which pretty much sums up the shortcomings of American education at every level. I explore Goodhart's law in Chapter 25.

Despite these obvious inadequacies, some teachers will follow the rules as closely as possible. If they're told to teach certain books, they'll teach those books and only those books. Such a conformist often receives rewards for sticking to the script even when the results are mediocre.

Others will spurn the rules by doing virtually the opposite. They'll teach as few of the prescribed books as they can get away with while trumpeting their own *contrarian* ways. They'll pretend to be free thinkers but are really just reacting to the same stimuli as their archenemy, the conformists. The only difference between them is that the conformist thoughtlessly complies with convention while the contrarian knee-jerk rejects it.

A third type, the *individualist* or maverick, will just light out on their own and do what suits them best. For instance, an individualist English teacher might teach a few books they want off the assigned list but will also teach whatever else appeals to them. They don't stick to the script unless it serves them personally.

With each of these types—the conformist, the contrarian, and the individualist—notice that the principal driver of what and even how they teach isn't necessarily what's best for the students but what's most comfortable for the teacher.

My friend Geoff, in contrast, decides what to teach and how to teach based on his assessment of his students' needs. He reviews the school district's curricular requirements, taking what he knows will work and discarding the rest while adding what he decides—in his professional opinion—will maximize his students' learning.

It's risky, frankly, even with his tenure and union protections, but—in the spirit of Gould's graduation charge to our class—Geoff can't stand to do anything less than right by his students, and he'll break every rule to do so. No surprise, but he's successful, too.

The day I watched him teach, I couldn't resist stopping one of his 11th-grade classes as they filed out to the squawking buzzer that announced the end of the period. I told them that their reading and responses to literature were at a level I'd expect from college sophomores. They, of course, were unimpressed by this weird old man's rantings.

Geoff, as a professional educator, thinks and behaves like an iconoclast. He's not mindlessly devoted to what he's told to do like a conformist. He doesn't mindlessly reject it like a contrarian either. Nor does he heedlessly inject his wants and needs into his pedagogy like an individualist.

No, Geoff starts with the student and ends with the student, and what unfolds in between is all about the student. Oh and by the way, his students have a spectacular track record on standardized tests, even though he violates every district diktat that gets in the way of actual student learning.

What Iconoclasm Has to Do with Leadership

What does all this have to do with leadership? Well, everything.

As I argue in Chapter 19, "every leadership challenge is a teaching challenge." Great teachers are also great leaders, and vice versa. Therefore, the connection between quality teaching and quality leading is inextricable.

Walter Bennis wrote that "Leading means doing the right things, and managing means doing things right." In other words, bosses who follow the rules to the exclusion of all else, like teachers who strictly adhere to the assigned curriculum, are conformists. It's impossible to impulsively conform and be a leader.

Same thing for contrarian bosses for the same reason. Conformists and contrarians are just two sides of the same coin, reacting to the same inputs but in opposite ways. Neither knows how to truly lead because they both focus on rules to the exclusion of all else—uncritically obeying them or instinctively disobeying them.

Similarly, individualists may show some independence and marks of leadership, but their self-serving tendencies forever stunt it. The arbitrary self-indulgence of the individualist is ultimately limiting or even damaging.

In contrast, true leaders look to and serve their people first to achieve real and lasting success, just as Geoff looks to his students to deliver what they need, not what he wants.

Great leaders will follow the rules so long as the rules remain sound and advantageous. Great leaders also readily bend or ignore the rules to benefit the greater good or serve the mission. Great leaders even intrepidly destroy the rules when they run counter to what's right. This adherence to practical iconoclasm was Gould's charge to my graduating class.

None of this activity is arbitrary since the actions of a great leader are always in service to their core values, the organization's mission, and the success of all. As we plainly can see, to remain most effective, great leaders must think and behave like iconoclasts.

Chapter 23: Gut Leadership Is Good, but Brain Leadership Is Better

"Intuition will tell the thinking mind
where to look next."

—Jonas Salk

Leadership is practically in my blood. From a young age, I have been thrust into leadership positions where I had to rely on my wits to succeed. Nonetheless, I always was a pretty good gut leader.

Picture this scene: a 12-year-old me, skinny, thick glasses slipping down my nose, and nerdy as hell. Somehow, I ended up in charge of my Boy Scout troop way before I was old enough. I was King of the Nerds even before I reached high school! We had our rough spots during my reign, but I had some fine moments as well.

A little jump ahead, and I'm 18 and a full-fledged boss, complete with employees (most older than me), a ton of responsibilities, and a gaggle of volunteers. My title was technical director of a small community theater, which meant I had to make sure we got the sets built, the lights lit, the sound balanced, and the flats painted. I made my share of blunders, but people followed me despite my tender age. This scenario has been a recurring theme ever since—leading, whether in an official capacity or just stepping up as needed.

Jump ahead a lot more, and I'm landing my first job as a professor. True to form, in no time I was a faculty leader at my university, chairing committees, running the faculty government, and even overseeing the university's reaccreditation process. Before I knew what was happening, I was a dean.

I'm not boasting when I say that I have innate leadership ability. It's just a fact, like being right-handed, and probably—like right-handedness—the result of me being my parents' son.

But my leadership instincts were never enough. Sure, I could navigate through challenges and get others to do what needed to be done, but I had no idea why. No big deal, right? It's not important to know why, right?

Wrong. It's a big deal. As my deanly responsibilities expanded exponentially, it dawned on me that gut leadership could only take me so far. Real leadership required more than intuition; much more. I needed to intentionally and fundamentally grasp the point of what I was doing so that I could know how to do it well and what to do next. And to pull that off, I needed to understand the *why* of leadership. Only then could I excel as a leader.

Beyond the Gut

Leadership is a skill, and like most other skills, while you might be born with some acumen, it must also be learned. The thing with learning new skills is that while someone can guide you through the process, they can't teach you to master the actual skill. That only comes through application and practice.

When my niece was very young, I played with her in the backyard. The game was for her to kick a rubber ball between my legs while I blocked with my hands. Boom! She kicked it so hard that it sailed over my head, over the large fence behind me, and into the next yard. She was four.

Fast forward, and there she is, being honored as one of the state's best high school soccer players. How did she get there? I'd love to say it was that makeshift backyard game with her uncle, but no. Nor was it only her innate athletic abilities, the same ones that enabled her to blast that rubber ball into orbit. The fact is that she took that raw talent and then worked her tail off. My niece's secret sauce was a blend of gut ability, dedication, and effort.

And I'm sure there were girls she played with and against who were also very good but didn't possess the same inborn athleticism. How did they succeed? Pretty much the same as my niece; they worked at it.

Leadership follows a similar formula. You can be born with some leadership prowess, but to succeed on the big stage, you must study leadership and apply what you learn. Even if you're not born with the knack, you can still learn it all the same. Either way, leadership—like soccer playing—is a lifelong discipline that requires mastery and upkeep.

The Necessity of Learning to Lead

Here's the reality, though. There's no point in learning leadership if you don't do leadership and don't continuously apply what you learn. Take my niece. If I told you she hung up her cleats, you wouldn't say she was a soccer player anymore, would you? She would become a former soccer player. Same for leadership. If you stop applying your skills, you cease to be a leader. That's true even if you retain a management title.

This insight may seem like a "well, duh" moment, but it's astonishing how often it's ignored. We see bosses who once knew how to lead but have since opted to just be bosses. Why? Maybe it's out of ego, laziness, or weakness.

Picture someone who once played soccer but hasn't touched a ball in years suddenly being thrust into the big game as team captain—chaos would follow. Same thing with all those ex-leader bosses. Mix them in with bosses who were never leaders to begin with, and it's no wonder that so many of us hate our jobs.

I make this same point in Chapter 15: *leadership is a lifelong discipline.*

It's not a temporary state or a one-time accomplishment. It's a continuous journey of learning, applying, and evolving. If you stop at any point, you're not a true leader—you only used to be. And let's be honest, don't we have enough bosses who pretend to lead while sowing nothing but chaos and misery? I bet you can name names.

It's time to break that cycle. Leadership is a commitment, not just a title. While it's possible to gain leadership skills through instinct or trial and error, that's not enough. Real leadership growth only comes through study and practice—an ongoing effort to improve. It takes genuine discipline, but anyone who has worked for a true leader knows that the rewards can be glorious.

Chapter 24: My Time in a Cult

> "I loafe and invite my soul,
> I lean and loafe at my ease observing a spear of
> summer grass."
>
> —Walt Whitman, "Song of Myself"

You probably don't know this, but for years, I was in a cult. With the perspective of time, I can now see it. How could I have been so easily duped? This cult was so subversive that its diffuse leadership remained largely unaware that it was heading a cult. Its leaders, in fact, often suffered the most from the cult's abusive practices, which—as true believers—they still endorsed. Anyone who openly resisted the cult was threatened with ostracism and destitution—cast out from the fellowship and forced to fend for themselves in the outside world. It was a pretty bleak cult, and it seems hard to understand its allure from this distance.

According to various experts, certain criteria define a typical cult. These experts don't agree on all the indicators or even their number, but they overlap significantly. An online article by Sasha Blakeley, titled "Cult Characteristics and Behaviors," captures some of the most commonly listed criteria, which I will use to describe my cult and demonstrate that it was, in fact, a cult.

1. A charismatic leader

My cult didn't have a leader per se. As I said, the leadership was diffuse and, therefore, all the more insidious. Instead, this cult slavishly followed and worshiped an unreasonable and impossible ideal that it treated almost as an entity. This ideal offered little appeal in itself, instead holding out tantalizing rewards that would allegedly flow from its adoration. All these rewards were materialistic. Real-life exemplars—the ideal's greatest adherents—were exalted far and wide. Many of these were well-known—household names even—who supposedly had gone from ruin to glory just by worshiping this ideal. This rags-to-riches narrative was typically exaggerated or even false. Still, it all made sense from within the cult and seemed quite plausible and deeply desirable.

2. Ideological purity

Since the cult followed an ideal rather than a person, purity of thought was essential. Anyone who resisted or opposed the cult or questioned the truth of its central dogma in the least was mocked, shamed, or shunned. Existence outside the cult risked perpetual lethargy and penury. You could even be denied employment and the ability to sustain yourself by openly defying the cult. The cult's reach was vast, making total escape impossible if you wanted to live and work in society.

3. Conformity and control

Everyone associated with the cult had to abide by its rules at all times. Although few, the rules had ramifications that could affect and regulate every moment of your day, where you spent it, who you spent it with, and what you did. The leadership would enforce the rules and discipline the worst offenders, but most enforcement came from the rank-and-file members of the cult themselves, who happily policed their own.

4. Mind-altering practices

Almost voluntarily, my fellow cult members and I would subject ourselves to practices that tended to sever our hold on reality. For instance, self-imposed sleep deprivation was so pervasive that members of the cult would literally compete to see who got the least rest. Confessing you had a good night's sleep would expose you to scorn. Insomniacs earned admiration and sometimes envy. To the cultists, the need for sleep was a weakness and an enemy of the central ideology.

Not surprisingly, as with other cults, substance abuse was common. Drugs were needed to counter the effects of sleep deprivation, and caffeine in all its forms topped the list. Some hardcore members preferred stronger stimulants, including alcohol and illegal substances, to get through the day. The abuse of these substances also dominated recreation time—a practice the most extreme cultists called "playing hard," as in the slogan, "Work hard, play hard."

5. Isolation and love-bombing

Cult members spent almost all their time with other cult members, even their off hours. Their friends, lovers, spouses, and extended family were rarely not members. Therefore, every conversation and interaction had at least a tinge of cultist propaganda and doctrine. Ironically, despite this immersive interaction with other adherents, the rigors of the cult's practice often resulted in the dissolution of meaningful social ties, such as lost friendships, separation from family, and divorce. The children of cult members frequently suffered neglect and worse, but their early indoctrination into the cult's beliefs was assured.

Love bombing—manipulating a person through overt but sporadic displays of attention and affection—started immediately when members were recruited to the cult and continued regularly. Given its stealthy nature, there was no formal or overt induction into the cult, but even fledgling signs of adherence would be met with effusive praise. With such encouragement, resistance soon broke down. The most zealous senior members usually received substantial rewards to ensure conformity and loyalty. It's important to note that these benefits could never compensate for the gargantuan toll their devotion demanded.

6. Us-vs-them mentality

Anyone who didn't adhere to the cult or profess and practice its ideals met with utter contempt or pity. They were considered ignorant and benighted souls or, less generously, degenerate sinners whose reprobate beliefs and lives were regularly renounced. Their very existence stood as a threat to the cult. Anyone attempting to defect from the cult would face certain abuse. I can assure you that some current adherents to my former cult are reading this and regarding me just this way.

7. Time and energy

Time and energy were offerings of the highest value to the cult. This meant that—besides sleep—self-improvement, outside interests, and even health were sacrificed, limited, or adapted to fit the cult's exacting standards. As a result, cult members' diets often featured ultra-processed foods, such as fast food and power bars, all high in carbs, particularly sugar. Such unhealthy food served as just another drug for cult consumption. In this sense, it was a death cult that didn't value the well-being or lives of its members or even its leaders. Everyone was expendable and replaceable, which made ongoing recruitment imperative.

8. Apocalyptic thinking

While not every cult is apocalyptic, and my cult didn't focus on end-times beliefs, such concerns always lurked in the background. Adhering to the cult's ideals allegedly helped stave off some vague coming disaster—personal or universal—that would ensue if members grew lax or allowed their minds to fill with doubts or distractions. We were doing "God's work," we were told, with the explicit warning that any other beliefs or practices constituted "the work of the devil" and threatened the world order as we understood it.

My Ongoing Escape

I can never escape the cult entirely. While I reject its tenets and see its ideals as ridiculous and its rewards as false, its doctrine and practices never leave my mind. What's more, due to its pervasiveness, it infiltrates every level of our society—from the classroom to the boardroom, from the basement office to the Oval Office—and infects our culture like a virus. Although insidious, it's held up as a sacred source of great virtue and used to excuse all manner of atrocious behavior.

My road to recovery has been long and challenging, and I relapse frequently, tempted by the example of so many others around me. But ever since I began resisting, I can see how my life has improved. Relationships have strengthened, I'm healthier, and the returns are great and varied, extending well beyond the material. I can now see the dishonesty of the cult, but I still struggle to remain free. Nevertheless, I know I'll never regret rejecting this cult.

Admittedly, this cult has achieved great objectives. It's responsible for forging much of our world—the good and the bad—and a lucky few have managed to reap the rewards somewhat commensurate with their sacrifices. Still, it has destroyed far more lives than it has improved. And much of what it has created could have been built through other means or wasn't worth building at all.

You may be surprised by all I've described. Perhaps you're wondering what could be the appeal of something so consummately horrible. Maybe you're confused, wondering how you don't know of this widespread, influential, and pernicious cult. Ah, but you do know it and know it well.

Perhaps you're a member and don't even realize it.

Perhaps you're unwittingly a leader.

Are you still unaware of what cult I've described? It's built on the belief that toil is—in and of itself—the highest virtue. That working for work's sake is the highest ideal. It's the cult of hard work and overwork.

Perhaps you already knew what I was describing.

Perhaps, although besotted by its lies as I was, you've come to realize you're a full-fledged member of this cult.

Perhaps you want to consider another way.

Doing so can be quite challenging, particularly when your colleagues are adherents and your employers are cult leaders. Nonetheless, it's vital to recognize your predicament. Step one, identify the problem as a problem. Step two, recognize that you're in control of the solution.

Now go take some time off. Get some much-needed rest. Lol-
lygag for a while. Goof off. Loaf. Enjoy time with someone you
love. You've earned it. Your work will still be there waiting for
you when you return. Or maybe not. So what?

Chapter 25: Soviet Nails, Goodhart's Law, and the Culture of Unintended Consequences

"The road to hell is paved with good intentions."

—Traditional Proverb

Have you ever wondered why even the best-laid plans can sometimes backfire entirely? One explanation might come from Goodhart's law, a principle that explains why well-intentioned schemes often lead to unintended consequences.

Goodhart's law states, "When a measure becomes a target, it ceases to be a good measure." Let's put that in plainer English—when we define success as a bar to hit, we tend to find ways to hit it no matter what. Let me introduce Salvucci's codicil to Goodhart's law: "When we make the measure a goal, people tend to game the system." This gaming of the system leads to those unintended consequences.

This law operates freely in many workplaces. For instance, some bosses treat time-on-task (a measure) as their prime performance target in lieu of actual productivity goals. Equating time-on-task with productivity may work in some limited manufacturing settings of yore, but it makes no sense in our present-day service economy.

Take the work-at-home phenomenon spawned by COVID-19. We can find much evidence that this more casual approach to working hours increases productivity and certainly saves resources. Therefore, it stands to reason that traditional workplace performance goals may have been hindering productivity all along, a conclusion predicted by Goodhart's law.

How the Soviets Nailed Goodhart's Law

A classic (if dubious) example of the unintended consequences associated with Goodhart's law comes from the old Soviet Union. Our tale begins with the Soviet central planners. These geniuses—as they were wont—demanded that factories significantly increase the number of nails they manufacture. In other words, they set a measure (number of nails) as a goal. What do you think happened next?

To meet this new demand, the factories simply made lots of useless tiny nails. Thus, they pounded their numerical goal—the sheer number of nails produced—but only in practice, not in spirit.

The central planners quickly got wise to this scheme and replaced the count-based goal with a weight-based goal—another measure. In response, the factories hammered out just a few giant nails, which were also useless. System gamed!

While the particulars of this story seem a bit fanciful, it's similar to what you see in many workplaces. Employees are often assessed based on their time at their desks. Because no one can give 100 percent effort 100 percent of the time, workers waste hours on trivial tasks or social media to meet the goal of hours worked. They look busy while eating up the clock.

It would be harder for them to game the system if their performance were gauged by actual output quality. Instead of using time as the goal, the actual caliber of their work could be their target. The workers would get more done, and their workdays would likely be more satisfying and maybe even shorter. Of course, implementing such a scheme would require sound leadership.

Goodhart's Law Goes to School

Our acculturation to this world of unintended consequences begins in school. For instance, we can see Goodhart's law in action in the overuse of standardized tests. Many teachers and institutions are largely assessed by their students' performance on these tests—a measure—so the game becomes "teach to the test." Developing vital skills, such as critical thinking and creativity, gets abandoned in favor of pushing test content.

In more extreme cases, individual teachers, schools, and entire school districts have been known to cheat on the tests. Whatever form these standardized testing scandals take, they're predicted by Goodhart's law and Salvucci's codicil.

It isn't just standardized tests, though. Grading itself has similar unintended consequences. Because grades (a measure) have become the primary goal of student education and are entirely transactional, grade inflation, grade grubbing, and cheating pervade the educational system at every level. Therefore, in adherence to Goodhart's law, grades themselves undermine the true mission of education: student learning.

As an English professor, I used to teach first-year honors students. The college designated these students as elite largely based on their superior high school grades. Not so fast, though!

In practice, and with few exceptions, I found these brainiacs remedial in some areas compared to the general population of students. Unlike their middling classmates, the honors students generally resisted higher-order thinking and were inherently risk-averse and dogmatic.

How did they get such good grades in high school? Many of these honors students specialized in figuring out and delivering just what their teachers wanted. They excelled at accumulating and regurgitating knowledge, which helped them rack up high grades without wandering far from their comfort zone.

Don't get me wrong, all these students were bright, hard-working, and serious-minded. They were potentially as capable as or more capable than their non-honors peers. But most adhered fervently to the goal of accumulating points rather than challenging their minds. Sadly, their approach was no recipe for success in my classes since I insisted students take risks and push themselves intellectually. Would you be surprised to learn that I wasn't very popular with the honors students?

Let's break it down according to Goodhart's law. Since the measure (high scores) was the primary criterion for admission to the honors program, the students simply had to perform to that measure to achieve success. It was grueling but not necessarily rigorous work. As Salvucci's codicil predicts, although the honors students generally prided themselves on their academic honesty, many of them were—perhaps unwittingly—gaming the system.

While the honors students were extreme, you can readily surmise Goodhart's law's impact on academic grading in general.

Goodhart's Law at Work

It's similar in the workplace, where we offer rewards of various sorts for meeting arbitrary measures in addition to hours worked. For instance, an employee may be evaluated solely on achieving certain sales goals or on performance snapshots. These reward structures engender unintended consequences, including mistrust, team dysfunction, risk aversion, stunted creativity, lowered productivity, or worse. Meanwhile, employees naturally try to game the system to get ahead, flaunting the goals set for them.

Goodhart warns against the practice of converting measures into goals, but doing so has become so ingrained and widespread that it has developed into a culture of unintended consequences. Organizations often assume that because they have rules attached to measures, the rules themselves must be sound, no matter how misapplied.

The result? Things keep going sideways—the very opposite of effectiveness. As the unintended consequences mount, the expectations lower. We may meet the measures but only at the expense of true success, a formula for mediocrity.

What's the effect of Goodhart's law within your organization? How much do people game the system? Do you work in a culture of unintended consequences? Consider the reward system in your organization. What are the measures of success, and what are the goals? If they're the same, what are the unintended consequences?

An organization that deliberately accounts for Goodhart's law will excel. Does your organization inspire the best in its people or just the most? Does your organization emphasize doing things the right way while suppressing or even penalizing doing things right?

If so, your organization may suffer the effects of Goodhart's law. And tell me, whatever will you do with all those Soviet nails?

Chapter 26: The Ear Is Mightier than the Mouth

Let me tell you about this truth my friend Jeff sprung on me a while back: "In any communication, the listener has all the power." That profundity has been tumbling around in my head ever since. It's a great way for leaders to think about communication. When it comes to delivering a message, the ear has it all over the mouth.

When we talk about power in relation to listeners, we usually refer to active listening, listening to understand, and other leadership listening techniques. That's all great stuff, but not what Jeff was getting at.

The truth is that when you communicate, whether through speaking or writing, you give all the power over your message to the audience. They then can receive it, reject it, ignore it, distort it, interpret it, misinterpret it, or whatever they want. They can love it, or they can hate it, and you can do very little about the situation, even if you're the boss!

In short, once you've delivered your message, it's no longer yours to control. Importantly, though, while you've lost control, you still have ownership over the message. You're still responsible for it no matter how it's received!

Let's call this phenomenon the "messaging paradox," the idea that no matter how much care you take in crafting and delivering a message, you forever own it but will never control it.

Take this very essay. My goal is to hook you with my ideas and my writing and engage you in an intellectual exchange. As an author, I have a degree of authority, but that authority evaporates the moment you read it.

In this moment, you have the power. You get to decide what to do with my piece. You can read it and just forget what I say or willfully misrepresent what you read. You can read something in it that I never intended. You can get caught up in the thrill of my incandescent prose and never even bother to suss out my meaning, or you can just move onto something else without a thought. You could just stop reading right here!

———Hey! Happy you're still with me!

Complicating matters further, your understanding itself can change! You can read my essay one way today and another tomorrow. Ultimately, the success of delivering my message depends less on my skill and rhetoric than on some lucky guesses about you, the audience. Your mood, interests, and biases shape your interpretation, and I have no control over any of that. Once my message escapes out there to you—in the wild, so to speak—my direct influence pretty much ends.

Of course, some people successfully manipulate audiences through communication, but there are no guarantees. Once they've delivered their beguiling message, all they can really do is hope. All I have is hope. And trying to reassert control over the meaning of my message may as likely go south as hit home.

Let me give you a great example of that. In 2023, the country singer Jason Aldean stirred up a humdinger of a controversy with a music video for his shitkicker ditty "Try That in a Small Town." The song extols the saintly virtues of "good ol' boys, raised up right" while the accompanying video runs footage of rioting urban—that is, largely Black—protestors. The apparent suggestion is that, unlike country folk, city folk are just not "raised up right." Given the video's imagery and Aldean's racially fraught past, some have seen his overall message as racist, which Aldean denies.

Whatever the truth, Aldean's situation exemplifies the messaging paradox. Having now delivered and thereby lost control of his message, Aldean's efforts to regain control over it backfired. Soon, bona fide and avowed racists started championing this supposedly non-racist song. It also doesn't help his cause much that the concert portion of the music video was filmed on the site of a notorious lynching. Nor did Aldean do himself any favors by claiming that "there isn't a single video clip that isn't real news footage," which is simply untrue.

He further defended himself by saying that his song is intended to evoke "the feeling of a community that I had growing up," which is also misleading since he came up largely in Macon, Georgia, not exactly a "small town." At any point, he could have just wisely accepted that while he forever owns his message and the controversy it has generated, he has no control over it and never will. But wisdom isn't Aldean's strong suit.

My point here isn't to razz Aldean. He's generated enough trouble for himself. Still, if the intent of his song and video wasn't racist, he still has a lot more explaining to do. Don't feel too bad for him, though. He wasn't—as some wags have claimed—"canceled," not by a long shot. According to *Forbes*, he made a bundle from the controversy surrounding this objectively terrible song and its racist dog whistle of a video.

What Aldean failed to grasp is that embracing the truth of the messaging paradox requires something he lacks: humility, which—ta-da!—is what this piece is really all about. Great leaders recognize and accept the humility inherent in not being in total control of their message but still owning its repercussions. So, the next time you have something on your mind that you want to share, the next time you have something you want to get off your chest, the next time you have some pearls of wisdom to impart, remember my friend Jeff's wise words: "the listener has all the power." It's the ear over the mouth every time!

That's the messaging paradox. You lose control the second you speak, but you still own the consequences—all the responsibility and none of the authority.

That, my friends, is a powerful message in itself—and humbling too.

Chapter 27: The Consequences of "If It Ain't Broke, Don't Fix It"

> "That's the trouble with government: fixing things that aren't broken and not fixing things that are broken."
>
> —Bert Lance

My first job out of college had me traveling around the country to teach learning skills at various schools. For one gig, I drove to a little town in Virginia named for the Powhatan, the region's Algonquins. Pocahontas was a Powhatan. (Wasn't it nice of folks to honor the people who had been pushed out by naming a rural outpost after them?)

Early on, I had some issues with the precise pronunciation of the town's name. The townsfolk tended to slur the three syllables into two, which I tried in my flat Yankified way: POW-tan. Having been corrected several times, I finally threw caution to the wind and twanged up my pronunciation to sound like them—PAOW-taaan—and that did the trick.

After conquering the town's name, my next challenge was comparatively slight. The left turn signal on my '78 Impala was blinking slowly, very slowly. Click … click … click, as opposed to the normal click-click-click. According to the repair manual, I needed to replace a relay in the fuse box under the dashboard. Easy peasy.

A local saw me working on the car and asked what I was doing. When I explained the click … click … click versus the click-click-click, he asked, "So it still works, right?"

"Well, yes, sort of," I replied.

He then responded with a bit of cornpone that was new to me with my Philly upbringing, drawling, "Well, if it ain't broke, don't fix it." I chuckled at the witticism and went right on fixing what wasn't broke. After all, "ain't broke" doesn't mean "couldn't be better."

In the decades since, as I've moved about, I've heard the same saying repeated by many as the folk wisdom of their particular region. I've met Southerners who declared it a down-home Southernism. I've known Midwesterners who hailed it as an example of heartland perspicuity. Some Vermonters tout it as a flinty New England witticism. I once even heard a Brit on the radio claim it as an ancient English maxim!

It turns out that the phrase's homespun authenticity is dubious at best, with clear origins only going back to the 1970's. In other words, it isn't some rural proverb whose wisdom has been time tested and passed on through the generations. Indeed, it's a faux folksy bromide popularized by one Bert Lance, a corrupt official in the Carter Administration.

But let's face it: while the saying taps into our longing for the imaginary "good ol' days" when everything just seemed to work better, it's as bogus as the nostalgia it evokes. Yes, I could have left my car blinker as is, moldering in a state between fully broken and not broke. Instead, I opted to spend a couple of bucks and exert some minor effort to make it work perfectly again.

If the Horse Ain't Broke

That incident took place in 1987, and in case it wasn't historic enough for you, let's go back somewhat further to illustrate the fuller implications of "if it ain't broke."

Humans relied on their feet or animals to carry them and their luggage for millennia. However odd that seems to us now, it was just the way it was. No one thought that their transportation system was broken because it wasn't. People didn't go on to invent steam engines, locomotives, and cars because equine and pedal transportation was broken. They did so because it could be improved upon.

"If it ain't broke, don't fix it" sounds seductively reasonable initially, but it's a reactive approach, a recipe for stagnation and the status quo. If it breaks, fix it and return it to its previous state. Otherwise, don't bother with it at all. This model has its own name in some industries: "break/fix." The break/fix model may be good enough to get you through the next quarter, but it won't help you surpass your bolder competitors over a year.

If we were to heed this pseudo-colloquialism throughout our species' existence, we'd never explore, seek improvement, or pursue new possibilities. No one would have invented the steamboat or trains, and certainly not the automobile. And speaking of automobiles, I would have never have gotten to replace the stupid relay driving me nuts by making the turn signal go click … click … click instead of click-click-click.

By the way, don't confuse "if it ain't broke" with another saying: "Don't mess with success," which is a far more sensible notion and has the added advantage of rhyming. "Don't mess with success" is all about not forcing change just for the sake of change, which is what "if it ain't broke" was probably originally aiming for but missed by a country mile. Fixing something that ain't broken but can be improved is the essence of progress.

The Saga of Percival: Inventor, Philosopher, Troglodyte

Let me set a scene for you.

A caveman hunches over his work, wielding his simple stone tools to smooth a segment of tree trunk so that it'll roll easily. His buddy approaches and offers a query using the grunts that comprise their common tongue. On the off chance you don't understand caveman Gruntese, I'll translate.

"By golly, my dear Percival, whatever are you on about there?"

Percival looks up from his invention and proudly explains how his wheel—humanity's very first—will efficiently traverse the countryside, aiding in the transport of people and goods while sparing their feet. "Henceforth," Percival excitedly tells his friend, "we will thus be able to convey superior loads at a further remove."

"Why, Percival," his friend furrows his cantilevered brow, "Conveying parcels across the vast landscape is strenuous enough as it is, do you not think? Whosoever would endeavor to increase such burdens?"

Percival finds his friend's query flummoxing.

"Say, Percival," his companion continues, "My grandpapa seemed quite fond of a quaint aphorism that just might befit this moment. He was known on certain occasions to ironically affect an uncultured dialect and aver, 'If it ain't broke, don't fix it.'"

Instantly, the manifest truth of this sage, faux-Neanderthal observation overwhelms Percival. He jumps up and declares, "By gum, Thaddeus! You are dead right!" The two friends immediately set about smashing Percival's primitive wheel into kindling and adding it to their already hefty firewood burdens to haul on the long trek back to their cave homes.

At that very moment, humanity's fate is sealed. Without the first wheel, there can be no automobile. And without the automobile, I would never have had the satisfaction of returning my

car signal to its click-click-click state from its previous click …
click … click condition.

Therefore, let's not shackle ourselves with the limitations of "if
it ain't broke." Embrace innovation, seek improvement, and
don't shy away from fixing what's not actually broken but could
clearly be better. After all, the possibilities that lie beyond just
"good enough" may be the most transporting discoveries of all!

Chapter 28: "Character is Destiny"—What a Crock!

> "It was gravity which pulled us down
> And destiny which broke us apart."
>
> —Bob Dylan, "Idiot Wind"

The Ancient Greek philosopher Heraclitus of Ephesus left us this morsel to ruminate: "Character is destiny" (ἦθος ἀνθρώπῳ δαίμων). It's a well-worn and venerable saying, but frankly, I just can't agree with him, at least not in our common understanding of his meaning.

As we learn in Chapter 17, character is the first of the core elements of leadership—the 4 Cs—along with communication, compromise, and collaboration. Your character consists of your values, habits, beliefs, experiences, and everything else internal that drives or limits your behavior. In his original saying, Heraclitus' use of the term "character" (δαίμων) likely referred to something quite different—more akin to a soul or a guiding spirit but with a dash of behavior.

My issue with Heraclitus' saying doesn't stem from the word "character," though, but from the word "destiny," which is best translated as "fate" (*ἦθος*). The concept of fate had more consequential and complex implications in Heraclitus' time than in ours, with the Fates (*μοῖρα*) being immensely powerful immortals in Greek mythology. Nonetheless, instead of wading into that quagmire, let's focus on our present-day interpretation of Heraclitus' adage and our understanding of the terms "destiny" and "fate."

Today, we can use *destiny* and *fate* interchangeably to signify a preordained future, but subtle distinctions arise between them. For instance, destiny is usually the more optimistic term: "It was her destiny to have a loving marriage and succeed in business." Fate is—well—more fatalistic: "The Titanic met its fate on its maiden voyage." Furthermore, we usually think of our fate as the consequence of some outside force. Meanwhile, your destiny is the route of your ongoing journey toward that fate, a journey you help shape. Therefore, fate is utterly fated, and destiny is not so much.

Here's where I part company with our usual interpretation of Heraclitus's maxim. "Character is destiny" plops all the burden of our outcomes onto our poor, beleaguered character as I defined it above. Indeed, character can significantly influence destiny, but it doesn't control it. For one thing, the start of life doesn't deal us all the same hand. One person may hold a measly jack-high at birth, while another starts life with four of a kind. Character can sway how we play those cards, but going from a "royal sampler" to a royal flush takes more than just character or even skill.

And yet, we regularly laud those dealt life's best hands from the outset and ignore or even denigrate those who struggle their whole life to achieve a mere ace high. And what of luck's role throughout the game of life? Even the sharpest poker player must have a little luck on their side—unless they cheat.

Similarly, our society favors individuals for their superficial characteristics over their character. That's why certain traits dominate power centers in our world. For instance, take a look at the current makeup of the U.S. Congress. Do we really believe that men—so overwhelmingly represented there—are that much better at governing than women? You can ask similar questions about CEOs of major corporations or analyze who tends to populate high-paying fields versus who mostly works in the low-wage service sector. And then there's the persistent gender wage gap. And don't get me going about racial disparities in representation.

It seems so obvious, but it bears repeating: distinctions such as gender or race have nothing to do with an individual's character. Nonetheless, our destinies are heavily directed from the outset—for good or ill—by such factors over which we have zero control. In this sense, identity is destiny.

In addition, much of destiny stems from the accidents that occur throughout a lifetime. If you've ever had to endure mass layoffs, identity theft, or errant meteors, what does your character have to do with that? The same is true for happier accidents, such as winning the lottery. Yes, the strength of your character will affect how you handle happenstance, but being of sound character isn't some woo-woo guarantee of a particular life-altering mojo.

In short, the suggestion that our character is the sole or even chief arbiter of our destiny puts too large a load on individual qualities as far as I'm concerned. Heraclitus' "Character is destiny" may sound comforting to some because it suggests we have agency, but trying to squeeze all the highs and lows of life into one little container called "character" is too much.

Here's another sad reality. Being of the most upstanding character can even backfire. Let's face it: few work promotions are due solely to virtue. Wherever you look, you'll find decent and competent humans slogging along just to survive while jerks and scoundrels are launched to the pinnacle of success. Need an example? Again, allow me to reference the U.S. Congress.

In fact, "Character is destiny," when taken to its logical extreme, can justify all manner of atrocities because it can give the impression that achieving dominance is itself a mark of virtue, which is just not true. For instance, belief in Manifest Destiny led to the displacement and slaughter of millions of Indigenous Americans. Would you claim that this barbarity—allegedly "destined"—resulted from a mass failure of character in the Indian population? Were their genocidal oppressors paragons of good character? "Character is destiny," as we interpret it, would suggest so.

At this moment we should pause to acknowledge a much-ignored truth: that bad is generally stronger than good, and that good must therefore be smarter and ever vigilant. It's a tough pill to swallow, I know. I've choked on it many times. The fact remains that those who stand by their values are as likely to face undue penalties as to receive adequate rewards. In this way, their strong character may actually shape their destiny, but for the worse.

I admit that I'm being a bit hard on poor Heraclitus, who's not even here to defend himself. Surely his wisdom got lost in translation, and important nuances have certainly been obscured by the cultural fog of time. But here's the thing: as we interpret it in the present day, his little saying, however pithy and superficially appealing, stinks.

If we pin all of life's twists and turns of destiny on personal character, we must be at fault whenever things go wrong, even things utterly out of our control. How, then, can we forgive ourselves? Our interpretation of Heraclitus leaves no room for even a little self-compassion, which is neither realistic nor fair.

We're not perfect. Nor should we pretend to be. Therefore, our personal character shouldn't bear every burden. Certainly, live your true values to the fullest, but don't expect that to be enough. Be sure to mix in a healthy dose of self-compassion when your destiny goes down some twisted byway. Indeed, the finest and strongest character always includes plenty of self-compassion.

Hmm. Now that I think about it, in that sense, perhaps Heraclitus wasn't so far off the mark.

Conclusion: The Only Legacy a Great Leader Needs

"My name is Ozymandias, King of Kings:
Look on my works, ye Mighty, and despair!"
—Percy Bysshe Shelley, "Ozymandias"

Have you ever thought about your legacy? When you're young, the world's your oyster. You have all the time in the world. It's the time to live for the moment, to seize the day. Today's the first day of the rest of your life. Life moves fast, so live it to the fullest. And on and on with the other cloying and unhelpful cliches.

Frankly, the young just don't care much about legacy, what with all that time they have left. Legacy is for the long run. It's a game best left to the gray-haired folks shuffling toward retirement.

But is that true?

In reality, legacy is the culmination of all your experiences and efforts throughout your life and not just who or what you are in the end. That means the sooner you consider legacy, the sooner you can start shaping yours.

Legacy is paramount for leaders. But a leader's legacy isn't about self-congratulation and ego-stroking. It's largely the result of leaders just doing what leaders do, making a significant impact that happens to reverberate long after they've left the building.

The Bucket Test: Wet Throughout

Perhaps you've encountered a poem by Saxon White Kessinger called "The Indispensable Man." Here's the second verse:

Take a bucket and fill it with water,
Put your hand in it up to the wrist,
Pull it out and the hole that's remaining,
Is a measure of how much you'll be missed.
You can splash all you wish when you enter,
You may stir up the water galore,
But stop, and you'll find that in no time,
It looks quite the same as before.

He's talking about the mark you leave behind when you depart a situation, which he claims is none at all. So what's the point of trying if we're all replaceable?

But wait! Great leaders know bunk when they see it. Sure, no one is or should be indispensable (indispensable individuals in an organization may indicate a broken culture), and true leaders don't really fret much over whether they're missed.

That said, great leaders—by default—leave a mark that will long outlast them. Not content with splashing around a bucket, they seek to transform the contents of that bucket for the better and maybe even upgrade the bucket itself before they go.

I'll leave off the bucket metaphor now, but leaders are in the business of transformation and improvement, which means that leaders are in the business of legacy, a legacy that can change the world.

The Legacy Challenge: More Than Just Marble and Name Plaques

When we think of legacy, we usually think of something easily recognizable or even tangible. In a family, legacy might take the form of a bequeathal, or offspring could be one's legacy. In business, legacy might take the form of a momentous innovation or some physical structure, such as a new suite of offices.

In higher education, I've noticed that most university presidents—like the pharaohs before them—are almost comically mad to erect at least one edifice that bears their name before they shamble off. Sometimes, this monument serves a purpose, such as a new library. Other times, it's pointless, like a campus bell tower. The presidents' immortality is assured—I suppose they imagine—by their name being affixed to the new building.

These physical memorials, though—as impressive and visible as they are—constitute a crude and superficial sort of legacy. Mere years later, the legacy of that name on the building will only inspire a half-interested "Who's that?" from the occasional passerby.

Now, we should turn to the legacies that truly matter—the ones that, unlike a new parking garage or an indoor pool, quietly and permanently shape the future. These legacies have nothing to do with stroking egos or physically defacing landscapes. These are the legacies that genuine leaders—the ones who really get it—naturally cultivate just by practicing good leadership, and they take two forms: establishing resilient systems sustained by healthy cultures and creating and empowering other great leaders. Although often invisible, such legacies are always invincible.

Systems and Cultures: One Aspect of Legacy

Let's start with creating systems and cultures.

Any half-decent manager can cobble together a functional system. But getting that system to work, keeping it running smoothly, and continuously improving it? That's the stuff of true leadership and is precisely where culture-building comes in.

An organization's culture determines whether its systems will function properly or at all. Think of a car engine. You can build and fuel the engine properly, and it'll start just fine. But to keep it running, you'll need to lubricate it with oil. That's culture—the Valvoline of workplace systems!

This healthy culture then regularly fosters strong values and inspires the best in everyone, keeping institutions going. Such cultures aren't only welcoming and encouraging, but they also cultivate creativity and progress.

When a leader establishes effective systems and the culture to sustain them, that legacy often outlives the leader. Even if their successor is just a placeholder or a dud, that newbie can still benefit from the systemic and cultural groundwork their predecessor laid.

Power to the People: The Other Leadership Legacy

The second type of legacy is more durable and has a much, much greater reach. This legacy revolves around people and the development of other leaders.

Simply put, great leaders beget other great leaders. Doing so is just a natural extension of being a true leader, and they do it in two ways:

One way is by example. The behaviors managers model can be contagious. If they act like jerks, then they'll preside over a culture rife with pettiness, egotism, control freakery, and such. In short, they'll be mere bosses. If they embody true leadership, they'll inspire others to trust one another enough to collaborate on mutual success. Such is the impact of example.

The second method is even more straightforward: through direct instruction. This is when leaders teach others the discipline of great leadership. They can use training, coaching, mentorship, and the like in any combination. This practice is intentional, sometimes formal, and always impactful.

Both methods—example and instruction—are needed to bring up new leaders. After all, example without instruction can only take you so far. And instruction without example just creates a counterproductive climate of "do as I say, not as I do." Such hypocrisy is anathema to leadership.

The Compound Interest of Leadership: Changing the World

The legacy piece kicks in when others find success as leaders themselves and spread the leadership ethos far and wide. Again, this legacy has nothing to do with ego. It's simply what great leaders do by default. Leaders inspire and bring up new leaders; they beget leaders. And those new leaders go on to beget even more leaders. And so on and on.

When you engender such a legacy of exponential leadership, it need not stay confined to your original institution. As new leaders fan out to new businesses, organizations, and even industries, the leadership ethos travels with them, indefinitely and without limit.

Imagine that pawn from our chess example in the introduction. From that one enlightened piece we see growth spread across the population of pawns, each one inspiring the rest on both sides of the board. Their growth challenges the supposed superior pieces—the knights, the rooks, the bishops, and maybe even the royals—to develop their own characters. Soon the four corners of this one board can no longer contain all that growth!

If all this seems a little overwhelming or even far-fetched, remember that creating new leaders is just a routine activity of being a leader. It isn't some lofty ideal or additional task listed under "other duties as assigned." It's already written in the virtual job description of great leadership. From there, such a leadership legacy operates much as compound interest does—small actions that grow massively to impact the future and change the world for the better.

The Leadership Challenge: It's Your Oyster

As a leader, contemplating your legacy isn't an exercise in self-indulgence. It's a crucial part of your role that demands immediate attention. What exactly are you doing if you aren't busy creating solid systems, cultivating positive cultures, and nurturing new leaders? I can tell you this: you're not leading.

No, great leaders are preoccupied with legacy, not out of self-regard but because leadership values and behaviors aren't one-offs. Leadership without lasting impact is no leadership at all because leaders, by definition and inclination, shape the future. They lead today to forge a better tomorrow.

So, get cracking on that legacy now, whatever your age. Look around. Institutions all over are desperate for new and better systems and healthier cultures. Even more chronically, the whole world is crying out for better leaders—we see it everywhere in every aspect of life. The minimum requirement is that you lead well. By doing so you'll create all the legacy you'll ever need. That's how we make a true difference in the world!

Author Bio

Jim Salvucci, Ph.D., founded Guidance for Greatness to help new leaders reach their full potential. After serving 30 years as both a professor and C-suite executive in colleges and universities, he knows what makes a leader great. Along with his university degrees, Jim trained in leadership at Harvard and the American Council on Education (ACE) and has earned several certifications in coaching. He's shared his unique ideas through TEDx and other talks around the world. While his distinctive approach might surprise you sometimes, Jim's guidance can help you become the leader you're meant to be.

Find more of Jim's ideas at *On Leading with Greatness* (jim-salvucci.substack.com).

www.ingramcontent.com/pod-product-compliance
Lightning Source LLC
Chambersburg PA
CBHW041558160726
48006CB00042B/2023